Thomas Withers

Observations on chronic weakness

Thomas Withers

Observations on chronic weakness

ISBN/EAN: 9783337730352

Printed in Europe, USA, Canada, Australia, Japan

Cover: Foto ©ninafisch / pixelio.de

More available books at **www.hansebooks.com**

OBSERVATIONS

ON

CHRONIC WEAKNESS.

BY

THOMAS WITHERS, M.D.

YORK:

Printed by A. WARD; and Sold by T. CADELL, in the Strand, and W. NICOLL, in St. Paul's Church-Yard, London.

MDCCLXXVII.

TO

Sir JOHN PRINGLE, Bart.

Phyſician in Ordinary to Her MAJESTY,

AND

Preſident of the Royal Society.

SIR,

I Take this opportunity of acknowledging my obligations to you, for your peruſal of a treatiſe lately publiſhed by me on the Abuſe of Medicine. I know that vanity is a weakneſs; yet I confeſs that mine was ſomewhat flattered by the favorable opinion you conceived of that publication, and the obliging manner in which you were pleaſed to ſignify it to me. The ſtudy of medicine, Sir, is one of my greateſt pleaſures; and I ſhould be happy to promote, in any degree, the fuccefsful practice of that ufeful and noble art. If, at the fame time, any production of mine fhould happen to afford the fmalleft entertainment in a leifure hour to a man of your character and talents, fo eminently diftinguifhed in the literary world, I fhall have attained a point beyond my expectation. It is, Sir, with fingular fatisfaction, that I have the honor of fending thefe few pages into the world under your patronage, and of fubfcribing myfelf, with all refpect and gratitude,

Your much obliged,
And moft obedient fervant,
THO. WITHERS,

York, March 14,
1777.

ADVERTISEMENT.

CHRONIC WEAKNESS is a frequent, diftreffing, and fometimes dangerous difeafe. It attacks perfons of all ages, of both fexes, of every temperament, and in every climate. It is accompanied always with anxiety, and often with fevere and lafting pains.

Chronic weaknefs is a term, which is fufficiently underftood by every one, who is in the leaft converfant with medical writings. It is a fpecies of weaknefs, which ought to be diftinguifhed from the fudden depreffion of ftrength, that occurs in fevers and other acute difeafes. Confidering the multiplicity of medical authors, it is not a little furprifing, that the fubject of chronic weaknefs fhould never have been fully and accurately difcuffed. The great Boerhaave, under the title of the relaxed fibre, touched upon the outlines of this

difeafe

disease in his elements of the practice of medicine. His learned commentator, Van Swieten, has enlarged upon the subject. But there are many important facts, relating both to the history and to the cure of this complaint, which are not to be found among their observations.

The author was at first induced to bestow particular attention on this subject, because he saw that several of his friends and acquaintance labored under the complaint, and he was anxious to relieve them. Success in a few instances was followed with an opportunity of practice in many others.—The author does not imagine that this essay contains any new observations on chronic weakness, which may not have occurred to men of large experience and extensive knowledge in the profession of medicine; but he hopes, that to others who have not had the most desirable opportunities of improvement, a more full and accurate account, than he has hitherto met with, of the symptoms of chronic weakness,

weakness, together with its causes, distinction, prognostic, and method of cure, will not be unacceptable.

Chronic weakness is not only a source of much misery in itself, but it lays the foundation for a variety of other diseases of the most fatal kind. Hence the necessity of a timely application of remedies for the removal of a disorder, which is productive of such unhappy consequences. This species of weakness is universally allowed by physicians, to constitute a most important part of the numerous chronic disorders with which it is united. The study, therefore, of chronic weakness, is a necessary prelude to the study of chronic complaints in general. The author of these pages intends, if his health and leisure will permit, to treat hereafter of several other diseases incident to the human body, and for this reason also, found it expedient to premise these observations on chronic weakness.

The

ADVERTISEMENT.

The author, confidering the nature and danger of the difeafe, was forry to find that it was fometimes looked upon as an unintelligible cafe, not to be diftinguifhed by any particular name. At other times he found it miftaken for the hypochondriac complaint, the hyfterical affection, a latent gout, a low nervous fever, and various other diforders which exifted only as effects of chronic weaknefs. In confequence of fuch miftakes, the practice was neceffarily imperfect, confufed, and erroneous. Sometimes it accidentally relieved, but often it increafed the malady. It was always unfteady, being regulated by no principles, and founded on no rational fyftem. By this means the difeafe, through imprudent treatment, was often rendered more obftinate, and even incurable.

The following obfervations have been carefully collected from a variety of cafes, both in private practice and in public hofpitals. Thefe cafes are ftill in the poffeffion of the writer, but it will be unnecef-

fary

ADVERTISEMENT.

fary and uninteresting to crowd the present work by entering into a minute detail of them. In selecting these observations on chronic weakness from the above-mentioned cases, the author has been particularly cautious to set forth every fact which might be conducive to health, and he has been equally cautious to suppress every idea of theory which, though capable of some support from sophistical reasonings, was not confirmed by experience, and might have led to pernicious practice.

CONTENTS

SECTION I

...

SECTION II

Causes of Chronic Weakness ...

SECTION III

Diagnostics and Prognostic of Chronic Weakness 52

SECTION IV

Method of Cure in Chronic Weakness, with respect both to Regimen and Medicines 92

CONTENTS.

SECTION I.

History of Chronic Weakness — Page 1

SECTION II.

Causes of Chronic Weakness — 18

SECTION III.

Distinction and Prognostic of Chronic Weakness — 55

SECTION IV.

Method of Cure in Chronic Weakness, with respect both to Regimen and Medicines — 77

CONTENTS

SECTION I.

...

SECTION II.

...

SECTION III.

Difficulties and Prophecies. Chap. I.

SECTION IV.

...

THE

HISTORY

OF

CHRONIC WEAKNESS.

SECTION I.

CHRONIC WEAKNESS, being a very common difeafe, merits great attention from the practitioners of medicine. The human race is fo much degenerated from its original ſtate of conſtitutional vigor, that perfect health is rarely ſeen; and the greateſt part of mankind are found to labor, more or leſs, under the ſymptoms of chronic weakneſs. The frequency of this difeafe is much to be regretted, when we reflect that it principally arifes from our own negligent and imprudent conduct. Men are not difpoſed to ſubmit to Nature;

‑ture; but they wantonly deviate from the laws prescribed by her for their welfare and happiness. Our manner of living is frequently unnatural, and differs widely from the rude simplicity of our ancestors. We are often indolent to an excess. We not only indulge ourselves in luxuries, but weakly think them necessary for the real comfort and enjoyment of life.—The disorder, that I am going to treat of, is one which afflicts mankind in a strange variety of forms, and conduces greatly to their misery and destruction.

The term CHRONIC is used here to distinguish this species of weakness from that which occurs in acute diseases. The one comes on suddenly; the other steals upon the patient by slow degrees. The depression of strength, consequent on febrile complaints, is often removed in a short time by the assistance only of a mild restorative diet. Chronic weakness, on the contrary, is difficult to remove, and its cure is generally found to be the work of time. Yet so efficacious are the remedies and regimen employed in the treatment of this complaint, that few patients would fail of obtaining considerable relief, if they had but sufficient resolution to pursue with steadiness those means of cure,

which

which the experience of ages has proved to be fuccefsful.—As far as the fubject will admit, I fhall enumerate the fymptoms of chronic weaknefs in that order in which they naturally occur.

Chronic weaknefs ufually begins with morbid affections of the ftomach and bowels. The functions of the alimentary canal are of the firft importance; but its ftructure is delicate and tender. Flatulence, acidity, heart-burn, coftivenefs, or colic pains frequently afford the firft figns of the approaching difeafe. A diminution of appetite and a flight dejection of fpirits foon occur. The mufcular ftrength is impaired, and the patient feels a languor and an averfion to motion. This difpofition to indolence continually grows ftronger, and a fenfe of wearinefs is eafily induced.

By degrees thofe fymptoms increafe, and the whole conftitution is more and more depreffed. The fimple folids are relaxed, and the nervous power is diminifhed. The uneafinefs of the mind, arifing from a debilitated ftate of the body, becomes more confiderable, and contributes much to accelerate the progrefs of the difeafe. The aliment is often taken without appetite, and is very imperfectly digested. The ftomach and bowels are diftended with air, and, in confequence of that diftenfion, they are thrown into convulfive contractions, attended with pain and anxiety. A confiderable quantity of limpid water, or of the acid and putrid matters contained in the ftomach, regurgitates frequently into the mouth. In this ftate of the patient there is fometimes a fenfe of palpitation in the breaft, with a fhortnefs and difficulty of breathing. The head, from the great connection which fubfifts between that part and the ftomach, is affected with pain and dizzinefs. The pain of the head in fome cafes is extremely conftant and fevere. The dizzinefs arifes fometimes to fuch a height that the patient ftaggers like a drunken man. The food, according to its nature, is apt to run too far into the acid or putrid fermentation, and to load the alimentary canal with acrid and offenfive matters. In this fituation of the patient, a diarrhœa fometimes takes place, which is a natural and falutary effort of nature. At other times obftinate coftivenefs and colic pains fupervene.

The action of the heart and arteries is greatly impaired, and the circulation of the blood is languid

languid and imperfect. The contractions of the heart are sometimes slow, but generally frequent, and always weak. The pulse of course is often feeble, irregular, and frequent. If the arterial system be under a state of contraction, and there be an inflammatory disposition in the habit, the pulse is small and contracted. This symptom occurs in young people of the melancholic or sanguine-melancholic temperament, who are particularly subject to the gout. The blood does not circulate with vigor, and scarcely enters the extreme capillary vessels, which are every where distributed over the surface of the body. Or if the blood enters those vessels, it almost stagnates within them, and gives the countenance a livid, bloated, and unnatural appearance. From this weakness of the circulation, insensible perspiration becomes languid, and the skin appears dry and contracted. As the nervous power and circulation of the blood are defective, the native heat of the body is diminished, and the patient frequently complains of an universal sense of coldness. In this condition he has frequent recourse to large fires and very warm cloathing, which relax the cutaneous pores, increase the irritability of the body, and render it highly obnoxious to the influence of cold.

The

The strength of the patient, in procefs of time, becomes still more depreffed, and a fenfe of heavinefs and laffitude is more eafily brought on, either by walking, riding, or any other gentle mufcular motion. From this effect an opinion is haftily adopted, that exercife is pernicious, and ought therefore to be avoided; and this opinion is the more readily complied with, as it perfectly coincides with the patient's inactive difpofition. In this ftate of the complaint, a moderate exertion even of mufcular ftrength exhaufts the nervous fyftem, deftroys the appetite, produces ficknefs, palpitation of the heart, and quicknefs of breathing.

The mind becomes as indolent as the body, and as incapable of almoft every fpecies of exertion. Its efforts are weak and fluctuating; its judgments various and undecifive. It is unfit for deep reflection or clofe attention to any particular fubject. The memory is greatly impaired, and not exercifed without a fenfation of uneafinefs. The affociation of ideas is often imperfect. Slight contradictions or fmall violations of the rules of ceremony and politenefs offend the patient, and induce a tranfient fit of grief or anger which leaves him dejected and exhaufted. The leaft feeming neglect is
fully

fully weighed, and sometimes mistaken for an intended affront. This weakness of mind often appears in persons whose natural temper is amiable and indulgent. Along with these symptoms we find timidity, dejection, or even despair to be the frequent attendants of chronic weakness. Such mental debility occurs in patients who were before remarkable for their firmness, vivacity, and acuteness of understanding. During this dejected state of the mind, the whole constitution is amazingly disturbed. The distribution of the blood and of the nervous influence is very unequal. The heart palpitates, the stomach and intestines swell with flatulence, and there is frequently a copious discharge of pale urine. At the same time we must observe, that it is not uncommon in this disease for the patient to have a mind unaffected by fear, in a bodily frame that is weakened and exhausted.

From the want of vigor in the brain and of greater force of circulation, obstructions of the menses frequently occur, attended with pains in the back and in the region of the womb. In some cases the menses do not make their appearance at the usual period of life. When they do occur, they are often irregular, and
accom-

accompanied with fever, pain, and anxiety. By confent of parts fpafmodic contractions of the bowels are induced. If there be a topical laxity of the uterine veffels, the fluor albus or copious irregular difcharges of blood, accompanied with fevere pains, are the common confequence. But it is well known, that a fuppreffion of the menfes, or too frequent and copious evacuations from the uterus, are always followed with confiderable depreffion of ftrength.

In this ftate of the conftitution, nutrition is very imperfectly performed. The animal oil is reabforbed; the blood-veffels are not fufficiently diftended; the flefh feems loofe and wafted; and the fkin is every where fallow. The countenance in particular exhibits a dry, palid, and unwholefome appearance. The eyes are dull and heavy. The tongue is white and covered with a vifcid matter. The uvula and velum pendulum of the palate, in fome cafes, are at times fo relaxed as to prove extremely troublefome. The lips lofe their color, and the breath, from the foulnefs of the ftomach, is often remarkably foetid. The extremities of the body are not unfrequently affected with anxiety, and an aching pain of a peculiar nature, diftinct

CHRONIC WEAKNESS.

diſtinct from chronic rheumatiſm. At other times chronic rheumatiſm occurs, which retards the cure and greatly diſtreſſes the patient. The joints affected with rheumatiſm feel, in conſequence of their weakneſs, cold and dry, when the reſt of the body is in a warm and natural ſtate.—The urine is various; ſometimes turbid and high-coloured; ſometimes pale; and from the relaxation of the ſecretory veſſels of the kidneys, it is often ſeparated in too large a quantity. This ſpecies of diabetes is commonly attended with thirſt and great diminution of ſtrength.—If a woman who labors under chronic weakneſs becomes pregnant, ſhe is, from the relaxation of the womb, very liable to miſcarry. The os internum of the womb ſometimes yields to the preſſure made upon it in a ſtate of pregnancy, and a miſcarriage is the conſequence.—As the patient can only take a ſmall quantity of aliment, and digeſt it but in a very imperfect manner, the blood is much impoveriſhed, and the ſerum bears too large a proportion to the lymph and red globular part. It is ſometimes owing to this unnatural quantity of ſerum in the blood, that the ſurface of the body appears tinged with a yellowiſh color; for the extreme veſſels neceſſarily exhibit an appearance upon the ſurface, fomewhat fimilar to that of their contents. When this fymptom occurs, without any obftruction of the liver, the ftools are of a proper color, and the paffage of the bile is free.

The patient is often afflicted with want of fleep. At other times, his fleep is interrupted, unrefrefhing, and difturbed with fudden wakings and frightful dreams. The anxious patient imagines himfelf, during his fhort and imperfect repofe, to be fometimes falling from a high precipice, to be fuffering punifhment for having committed the moft horrid acts of injuftice; or, by fome unforefeen misfortune, to be plunged with his whole family into the moft diftrefsful fituation.

The organa virilia are in a weakened and relaxed ftate. There is frequently a difcharge of thick vifcid mucus from the urethra and veficulæ feminales. The teftes are affected with tranfient pains, and a rotatory motion. A fmall quantity of femen proves too great a ftimulus to the relaxed feminal veffels, and confequently fomnia libidinofa & emiffiones nocturnæ are very frequent *. If the relaxation of thofe parts be ftill greater, evacuations of femen, fine penis tentigine, occur at uncertain

* Pathol. Inftit. Gtub. § 562.

CHRONIC WEAKNESS.

tain times, which weaken the conſtitution as much as they depreſs the ſpirits.

The hemorrhoids are a troubleſome ſymptom in this complaint. A languid circulation, a relaxed ſtate of the hemorrhoidal veins, and a coſtive habit of body, together with the natural depending ſituation of thoſe veſſels in a looſe cellular membrane, favor the frequent occurrence of the piles. Sometimes there is only pain and ſwelling without any evacuation of blood. At other times the evacuation is conſiderable, and conduces not a little to haſten the fatal termination of the diſeaſe. In ſome caſes, neverthelefs, the patient, if he previouſly labored under a venous plethora, finds a ſenſible relief in conſequence of a moderate diſcharge of blood from the hemorrhoidal veins.

Of all the parts of the body, the circulation of the blood through the vena portæ is the ſloweſt. For in diſtributing a certain proportion of blood through the liver, nature deviates from her ordinary courſe, and ſupplies the place of an artery by a vein, which divides itſelf into innumerable branches through the ſubſtance of that glandular body. It was neceſſary that the blood ſhould move on ſlowly, in order to ferve for the feparation of a fufficient quantity of bile. But if the circulation through the liver be flower than is natural, obftructions and biliary concretions are apt to occur *. In the advanced ftages of chronic weaknefs thefe fymptoms are not uncommon, accompanied with pain in the region of the liver. In this cafe a yellownefs of the fkin is obfervable, arifing from an obftruction of the biliary ducts and a reabforption of the bile. The patient is coftive, the ftools are whitifh, and the urine is high-coloured. As foon as thefe bilious fymptoms appear, they are too often confidered as the original difeafe, and the cafe is, without foundation, treated entirely as a jaundice. The biliary fymptoms are only the confequence of chronic weaknefs, and though they require a particular treatment, they are by no means to be regarded as the primary complaint.

In this relaxed ftate of the general conftitution, and particularly of the alimentary canal, worms frequently occur as a fymptom of chronic weaknefs. The fuperabundant quantity of mucus, lodged in the ftomach and bowels, forms a convenient nidus for the rife and encreafe of the different fpecies of worms. This fymptom

* Pathol. Inft. Med. § 515.

CHRONIC WEAKNESS.

symptom occurs more frequently in children than in adults. In consequence of an erroneous notion, that worms are the original complaint, and that the proper treatment is by purgative remedies, chronic weakness is often dangerously encreased, the constitution is greatly reduced, and, along with the worms, the patient is nearly destroyed. In this case the cure unfortunately proves far more dangerous than the complaint, which it was intended to remove.

In the progress of this disease the symptoms of hectic fever sooner or later make their appearance. The stimulus of a small quantity of food, particularly if it be of a heating nature, has a considerable effect on a weakened constitution. It excites the action of the heart and arteries, quickens the pulse, and produces a flushing of the face, with a sensation of great warmth in the palms of the hands, and sometimes in the soles of the feet. The febrile paroxysm, which naturally occurs in the evening, is encreased. It generally comes on before midnight, and after having continued for some time, terminates in a copious flow of the perspirable matter. It is sometimes preceded with a regular cold fit. Quickness of pulse, an un-

natural

natural heat of the body, and a fenfe of anxiety, are fymptoms which prevail during this febrile affection.

The irritability of the fyftem encreafes, and becomes a fource of much uneafinefs to the patient. The fmalleft furprize produces violent agitations both of the mind and of the body. An unexpected incident in even trivial matters will occafion a general tremor of the nerves, and excite the periftaltic motion of the ftomach and bowels to fuch a degree, as immediately to bring on vomiting or a diarrhæa. A flight application of unaccuftomed cold has the fame effect in exciting the action of the alimentary tube, increafing its evacuation, and aggravating all the fymptoms of chronic weaknefs. The fall of a poker or the fudden fhutting of a door is often acutely felt, and produces a troublefome emotion of the animal frame. The unexpected fight of an intimate acquaintance diforders the nervous fyftem. The depreffion of fpirits occurs more frequently and in a much higher degree. The falivary glands are fometimes affected in fuch a manner, that the faliva is fecreted as copioufly as if the patient was in a falivation from the ufe of mercury. The ftomach is often fo weak and irritable,

table, that even a small quantity of food cannot be retained; it occasions sickness and vomiting. As the periftaltic motion of the bowels is generally languid and weak, the body is usually coftive; but in some cases of particular irritability, the periftaltic motion is irregularly encreased, the aliment paffes through the inteftines in a crude ftate, and the ftools are loose and frequent, occurring for the moft part soon after the stomach is acted upon by the ftimulus of fresh food. The contractions of the heart and arteries become weaker, quicker, and more irregular, and the patient is subject to frequent faintings. The exhalant veffels, in the laft ftage of the difeafe, lose their contractile power; nocturnal sweats and a colliquative diarrhæa occur; serous fluids are sometimes effused into the cellular membrane and cavities of the body; the legs, the hands, and the face swell, and various dropsical symptoms appear, attended with violent pains of the abdomen. These hydropic affections arife from general weakness and relaxation of the syftem, and are the laft fatal marks of a broken conftitution. Thus the patient, after an uncertain term of years, is exhaufted and deftroyed.

Thefe

These are the symptoms of chronic weakness, carefully collected from a variety of cases, which have fallen under my own observation. The facts here enumerated are taken from nature, and ascertained by experience. The symptoms of chronic weakness occur in very different degrees, and I believe they are never all to be observed in the same patient. Some one part of the body is in general more afflicted with the disease than other parts. The head, the heart, the stomach and bowels, the kidneys, the womb, or the organa virilia, are frequently the principal seat of the complaint. In this case the patient is apt to overlook his less painful sufferings, and to dwell chiefly on those morbid affections, which he finds or which he thinks to be the most distressing. Being thus habituated to view his complaint as confined principally to a single part, that part, by this very circumstance, is apt to be more disturbed in the performance of its functions[*], and a fixed topical weak-

[*] Dr. Cullen and Dr. Fordyce are of this opinion. I was informed the other day by a learned and worthy gentleman, who was afflicted with a relaxation of one of the upper eye-lids, that whenever he thought most of his complaint, it proved the most troublesome to him. I was acquainted too with a gentleman who was a great hypochondriac, and labored under chronic weakness, who was apt to have giddiness in

weaknefs is induced. For the pernicious influence of an anxious mind may be extended not only to particular organs, but even to particular parts of the fame organ.

in his head, palpitation of his heart, diftention of his ftomach, or uneafinefs in his teftes, according as he fuppofed one or other of thofe parts to be morbidly affected.

C. THE

THE
CAUSES
OF
CHRONIC WEAKNESS.

SECTION II.

IT is probable that the immediate and PROXIMATE CAUSE of chronic weakness consists principally in a want of nervous energy, in an encreased mobility of the nervous system, and in a diminished cohesion of the particles of matter which constitute the simple solids. The proximate cause, as here stated, seems to be confirmed by the symptoms of the disease; and indeed it consists of facts, the knowledge of which is of the first importance in regulating the cure. The softness and relaxation of the simple solids, the
weakness

weakness and irritability of the moving powers, the dejection and timidity of the mind, are the natural consequences of such a morbid state of the constitution. The mind and body being so intimately connected, the disorders of the one greatly affect the health of the other. From this proximate cause too arise all the signs of languor and debility in the vascular system and in the alimentary canal. The affections of the womb are readily accounted for upon the same view of the disease. From the emptiness of the constitution, and the diminished vigor of the circulation, the evolution of the uterine system is imperfect, and a sufficient congestion of blood in the uterine vessels does not occur. Hence a want of the menstrual evacuation at the period of life in which it usually takes place, or a suppression after it has made its appearance. The too copious and irregular discharges of the menses arise from topical weakness and relaxation of the uterine vessels. But it is needless to go further into the explanation of all the symptoms of chronic weakness, which upon the principles here laid down are obvious in themselves, to any one tolerably acquainted with the institutions of medicine. We shall therefore proceed to the consideration of the PREDISPOSING and OCCASIONAL causes of the complaint. The enumeration of thefe, and the method of treatment, will ferve to illuftrate our doctrine concerning the proximate caufe. The occafional caufes are fuch as weaken the nerves and relax the whole conftitution, and the method of treatment confifts chiefly of the application of thofe means, which are efficacious in reftoring the enervated fibres to a ftate of vigor.

Chronic weaknefs is an hereditary difeafe. Weak parents have often the misfortune to fee a weak and fickly offspring. Though the infant fhould apparently thrive and flourifh a while at its firft entrance into life, yet, like a plant growing in too fhallow a foil, it often droops and pines away before it arrives at a ftate of maturity. Old and debilitated fathers, funk with the infirmities of luxury and debauch, can hardly expect to be bleft with children whofe conftitutions are vigorous. The ftamina of life are not of a durable kind, and the fruit will necessarily be imperfect. It is a melancholy reflection to a feeling mind, that the weaknefs and difeafes, which arife from indolence, ignorance, and imprudence, fhould be entailed upon our pofterity.

CHRONIC WEAKNESS.

A peculiar delicacy and tenderness of the animal fibres predisposes to this disease. Those who are born with such fibres are injured by flight occasional causes, and are more frequently afflicted with chronic weakness. Persons with light hair, a very fine skin, and a fair complexion, have in general a great delicacy of bodily structure. This temperament, like all others, is founded on the original stamina of life. It is very commonly attended with an irritable state both of body and mind.

Too great fulness of blood distends the vessels beyond their natural tone, and impairs in time the vigor of their contractile power. Nothing is more common than to see, in a course of years, the most healthful constitutions broken and destroyed from this single cause. A miserable train of symptoms, attended with great anxiety of mind and uncommon depression of the vital powers, is sometimes induced by plethora. This cause acts slowly, but its effects are generally certain, and it reduces the most vigorous constitutions to a state of great debility and relaxation. The common causes therefore of plethora become indirectly the causes of chronic weakness. Full living is remarkably injurious to health, and continually proves the

the bane and mifery of thoufands. Excefs of animal food has a powerful effect in bringing on the plethoric ftate. For animal food is confiderably more nutritious than vegetable, and therefore is improper to form the principal part of the diet of ftrong people, who ufe little exercife. From neglect of this precaution, venous plethora in the decline of life is often induced, which is apt to be dangeroufly encreafed by the fuppreffion of the menfes, the fuppreffion of the hemorrhoidal flux, or of any other ufual evacuation. Weaknefs of the conftitution from plethora, in confequence of full living, is of a very obftinate nature, and extremely difficult to remove.

Neglect of exercife is another caufe of chronic weaknefs, and it is as powerful as it is univerfal. Nature intended man to be active, and he cannot deviate from her laws without materially injuring himfelf. A moderate degree of mufcular motion is neceffary for the due performance of the different functions of the body. Different degrees are requifite for different conftitutions. Even infancy and age cannot be preferved in a ftate of health without gentle exercife, proportioned to their ftrength. In confequence of the neglect of exercife enumerable

rable evils enſue. The nervous energy fails, digeſtion and nutrition are imperfect, the blood and other fluids are vitiated, the circulation is languid, the muſcular ſtrength is impaired, and the various ſymptoms of chronic weakneſs gradually come on.—Theſe ill effects are more certain if ſolitude be conjoined with indolence. Man is a ſocial creature, and the rational enjoyments of ſociety afford him one of the higheſt pleaſures in life. In ſolitude the patient is apt to brood over a ſlight indiſpoſition till he has magnified it into a dangerous complaint. Thus the mind becomes habituated to dwell upon the diſeaſe, which circumſtance indeed tends much to encreaſe it.—From theſe facts it is obvious that all thoſe profeſſions which lead to a ſedentary life are of an unhealthful kind. For ſuch is the ignorance or inattention of many, that they will indulge an indolence of diſpoſition as far as they are able, provided that indulgence does not interfere with what they call a prudential regard to their temporal intereſt and ſucceſs in life. They pay no attention to their health, till they have loſt that bleſſing for which nothing can compenſate. Some who have unhappily fallen into this erroneous practice, preſume even to cenſure the conduct of others who wiſely follow a different plan.

plan. They confider them as negligent in their profeffions. They forget that health is neceffary to the fuccefsful performance of bufinefs, and that moderate exercife is neceffary to the prefervation of health. Fatal experience too often convinces them of their miftake.

Sudden and violent exertions of ftrength tend alfo to enervate the body. Over-diftention and too fevere action of the mufcular fibres proves very pernicious to the nervous fyftem. Nothing is more powerful in deftroying the tone of the living folids, and inducing an obftinate degree of weaknefs. For by this means the action of the ftomach, the digeftion of the aliment, and the procefs of nutrition are greatly difturbed. Severe exercife or labor diforders the circulation, vitiates the quality of the fluids, difturbs the fecretions, produces copious fweating, forces and weakens the exhalant arteries, and does great injury to the conftitution. The lower clafs of people are very apt to run into thefe errors, and imprudently to deftroy their health. But they fhould know that all violent labor, and all endeavours to lift great weights, or in any way to exert their whole bodily ftrength, are extremely dangerous and abfurd.

Though

CHRONIC WEAKNESS.

Though sleep is absolutely necessary to the performance of the various functions of the animal economy, yet the nervous power is capable of sustaining life for a certain time without it. Afterwards a new supply of nervous energy is required, which can only be obtained by sleep. Want of sleep destroys the tone of the nervous system; it produces paleness, languor, coldness, indigestion, a weak circulation, and dejection of spirits.—From these facts it is obvious that all public routs, entertainments, and assemblies of every kind, at which the company keep late hours, and convert night into day, contribute greatly to the destruction of health. Nothing can in any measure compensate the loss of the natural hours of rest, but the unnatural conversion of day into night.—It is the want of sleep too that renders every profession and employment unwholesome, in which men are disturbed at the usual hours of rest.

The compression of any important organ is highly injurious to health, and is a common cause of general weakness. The different parts of the body are so exquisitely adapted to each other, that health is the necessary result of the natural action of those parts. Every bufinefs therefore that requires a particular pofture of an unwholefome kind, and fubjects the workman to compreffion, is to be confidered as a caufe of chronic weaknefs, which is more or lefs powerful in proportion to the degree of compreffion, and to the importance of the organ compreffed. A moderate compreffion, continued for a great length of time, will be productive of very pernicious effects. The pofures of children, if not particularly attended to, are apt to be of an improper kind. They fometimes make too frequent ufe of the fame pofition, till they have produced a curvature of the fpine. Strong flays are very unfit for children, and often occafion crookednefs and difeafe. Women who lace their flays in fuch a manner as to be difagreeably tight, comprefs the moft important vifcera, and greatly injure their health. Dr. Hunter, in his excellent courfe of Anatomical lectures, gives inftances of ftomachs whofe fhape has been rendered unnatural by the compreffion of flays. The unfortunate lady, who weakly facrifices her health to her vanity, will find to her great difappointment that fhe will not only lofe the real beauties of nature, which fhe might otherwife have poffeffed, but will be afflicted with pains of the ftomach and bowels, with heart-

burn,

burn, acidity, indigestion, low spirits, obstruction of the menses, bilious complaints, disorders of the lungs, relaxation of the nerves and many other troublesome symptoms of chronic weakness.—The effects of this species of compression, when a woman is pregnant, are still more pernicious. I have known some women in this state who have laced themselves so tight as greatly to endanger their own lives, as well as the lives of their children. Sickness, want of appetite, indigestion, colic pains, drowsiness, &c. are the frequent but smaller consequences of such imprudent practice during pregnancy.

Impure air has a very considerable effect in weakening the constitution. A constant supply of good fresh air to the lungs is necessary to health. The want of it is often attended with depression both of strength and spirits. The air of large towns is impregnated with smoke, putrid vapours, and various other impurities; and consequently is by no means so strengthening and refreshing as country air. Hence we find numbers of people who suffer materially in their health, when they are under the necessity of living some time in the unwholesome atmosphere, which perpetually surrounds the great metropolis of this ifland. Impure air is a caufe of chronic weaknefs, which, tho' fometimes flow, is always certain in its effects. Upon this principle it is evident, that all thofe trades and employments where men breathe an air loaded with duft, fteam, acids, putrid or mephitic vapor, exhalations from noxious metallic fubftances, &c. may without hefitation be pronounced unwholefome. For this reafon the profeffions of grinding corn, dreffing flax, brewing, tanning, painting, working in lead mines, burning charcoal, preparing vitriol, &c. are found to weaken and diforder the conftitution. Moift air is relaxing, and weaknefs is obferved to occur in a higher degree in wet feafons and in low marfhy countries. The action of the air upon the human body in preferving life feems not to be perfectly underftood. Some have imagined that we receive a fpirit of a peculiar nature from the air; but this is merely a conjecture. It is more certainly known that we throw off with the air a poifonous matter from the numerous exhalant arteries of the lungs. We find that air, when it has once ferved the purpofes of refpiration, extinguifhes flame, and proves fuddenly fatal to animals which breathe it. As the whole mafs of human blood circulates through the lungs,

CHRONIC WEAKNESS.

a confiderable quantity of this deleterious vapor is perpetually exhaling. Hence the air in all public places, where there is a large concourfe of people, is loaded with this noxious vapor, and confequently unfit for anfwering fully the important purpofes of refpiration. Small rooms, when crowded with company, are foon filled with unwholefome exhalations, unlefs the doors and windows be frequently opened to admit frefh air. To fleep in a fmall room with the curtains clofe is, for the fame reafon, very unhealthful.—But it would be an endlefs tafk to point out all the fources of impurity in the air. After thefe general remarks, it will not be difficult for any one to afcertain many other particular inftances of a fimilar nature. We cannot however neglect in this place the opportunity of acknowledging the great advantages which may be derived to fociety, from the ufeful experiments of the learned Dr. Prieftley on the fubject of air.

Too copious a flow of the milk impoverifhes the blood, and diminifhes the vigor of the conftitution. Milk is found to bear a ftrong refemblance to the chyle. If the nutritious parts of the blood, inftead of fupplying nourifhment to the body, pafs off in too large quantity by the fecretion of the breafts, thirft,
head-

head-ach, indigeftion, lofs of appetite, decay of ftrength, palenefs, failure of fight and wafting of the flefh are the common effects. Thefe morbid appearances will more certainly take place in conftitutions previoufly weak and delicate; for when women of relaxed fibres give fuck for any length of time, a greater degree of weaknefs, accompanied with hectic fever, is fometimes induced. Yet it is very improper and even dangerous for the fecretion of the milk to be fuddenly fuppreffed after delivery, by the rafh efforts of a miftaken art.

Excefs in venery is one of the moft powerful caufes of chronic weaknefs, and often induces a miferable degree of the complaint. Palenefs, languor, coldnefs, averfion to motion, lofs of appetite, diminution of fight, head-ach, vertigo, indigeftion, feminal weaknefs, tremor of the nerves, leannefs, and pains in the back are the common confequences of this caufe. Immoderata feminis profufio, non folum utiliffimi humoris jactura, fed ipfo etiam motu convulfivo, quo emittitur, frequentius repetito, imprimis lædit*. Great inequality of conftitutional vigor between perfons in the married ftate frequently gives rife to this difeafe. To indulge in lafcivious ideas

* Pathol. Inft. Med. § 562.

ideas and to run into a wanton excefs of venery, is as miferably ruinous of health as it is below the dignity of reafon. Onanifm proves the fad deftruction of many; for in confequence of that pernicious practice, the organa virilia are affected with a moft obftinate fpecies of weaknefs.

Too great heat relaxes and enervates the animal fibres. It is a moft univerfal caufe of chronic weaknefs. The chillnefs which occurs at the commencement of febrile diforders, has led mankind to be too cautious in defending themfelves from the influence of cold, and too indulgent refpecting the free application of heat. A great degree of warmth renders the body extremely weak and irritable, and very obnoxious to the action of cold.—The lungs are particularly injured by living in too warm an air. From this caufe the patient, efpecially if the cheft be narrow or the lungs obftructed with tubercles, is fubjected to frequent attacks of the catarrh, to habitual wintercoughs, and to fatal confumptions.—The influence of a moderate degree of cold is injurious to thofe only, who are too much expofed to a heated atmofphere. All trades and employments, fuch as making glafs, working

ing in forges, cooking victuals, &c. which expose men to excessive heats, are very dangerous to health. The removal from a temperate climate into a very warm one, gives often a severe stroke to a good constitution, and contributes not a little to bring on the symptoms of chronic weakness. Such a sudden change of climate determines the blood powerfully to the surface of the body, and leaves the larger vessels in a proportionable degree of emptiness, which state is accompanied with a sense of debility. Hot rooms, stoves, large fires, and too many cloaths are perpetual enemies to health. Too much heat impairs the strength of the nervous system, diminishes the tone of the stomach, relaxes the simple solids, and destroys the contractile power of the cutaneous pores. It is very unwholesome to be overloaded with bed-cloaths. The heat of the body in that case is closely confined upon its surface, and sweating is unnaturally promoted. The habit of sweating, however induced, disturbs the equal balance between what is taken into the body and what passes off by the different outlets. In health, the force of the heart and arteries is wisely proportioned to the contractile power of the cutaneous vessels. If, by excess of heat, the equilibrium be destroyed, a diseased state

will

CHRONIC WEAKNESS.

will neceffarily follow.—The imprudent application of heat in the treatment of acute diftempers, has been productive of violent fweating, which, if it did not prove fatal, was always fucceeded by great debility and relaxation.—The too frequent ufe of the warm bath relaxes the nervous fyftem and the mufcular fibres. The Bath waters are often extremely abufed, and recommended in difeafes which they evidently encreafe.—The various methods of applying vapor or warm water to the human body, as invented by Dr. Dominiceti, require the greateft caution and judgment to regulate their ufe in the cure of difeafes. In many cafes fo powerful a remedy may be employed with efficacy and fuccefs; but an indifcriminate application of it would certainly be attended with the moft fatal confequences to fociety.

All thofe caufes which weaken the ftomach, deftroy eventually the tone of the whole fyftem.—Over-diftention of the ftomach occafions great weaknefs in that organ. From this caufe, its fibres lofe their ftrength of contraction, the digeftion of the aliment is impaired, the nutrition of the body is defective, the appetite fails, and the vigor of the conftitution is deftroyed. To load the ftomach with too large a quantity

quantity of food is extremely unwholefome, and productive of various complaints. It is a common error, and ought to be carefully corrected. It is particularly hurtful when the aliment is of a firm texture, of a glutinous nature, of flow folubility, and confequently of difficult digeftion.—Hard drinking is a very frequent and fatal caufe of weaknefs in the alimentary canal. Wine and other fpirituous liquors, from their ftimulant and fedative powers, are capable of injuring, not only the ftomach and inteftines, but alfo the brain and nerves. Taken with too great freedom, they at firft excite the action of the fyftem to an unnatural degree. This excitement is followed by weaknefs and depreffion of ftrength. To be frequently intoxicated is miferably deftructive of health, and to drink freely is a practice that can by no means be indulged with impunity.—We may therefore affirm, upon the whole, that a ftimulating diet to a healthful conftitution is unnatural and pernicious*. Full living and the too liberal ufe of generous fermented liquors encreafe the quantity of the fluids, and induce plethora, which ftate, as we have before faid, is a frequent and powerful caufe of weaknefs. All high-feafoned things are unwholefome. They err greatly
who

* Haller. Prim. Lin. p. 342.

CHRONIC WEAKNESS.

who are of opinion that a man may indulge his appetite at pleasure, if he observe but rules of moderation with respect to the quantity of his food. Pepper, mustard, ginger, mace, and many other spices are too stimulating to be freely employed with safety to the constitution. The stomach, from their too liberal use, becomes accustomed to an unnatural stimulus, and by habit is rendered unable to perform its function without them.—The sedative quality likewise of tea and coffee injures the tone of the stomach and weakens the nervous system[*]. The heat of the water is also pernicious. If the water be hot, it hardens the fibres of the stomach and destroys their texture.

From the various excretory organs of the human body, a continual waste both of solids and fluids takes place. The friction of the fibres one upon another alters the cohesion and disposition of those particles of matter, which constitute the human frame. A fresh supply therefore of solids and fluids is constantly requisite, not only to assist the growth of the body, but to repair the losses which that body sustains in performing the ordinary functions of life. If that supply be not properly made,

[*] Percival's Essays, vol. I. p. 129.—Ibid. vol. II. p. 128.

made, langour and weakness will ensue. A want of food, or food of an unwholesome kind, must necessarily disorder the constitution. Against excess of aliment, nature is provided with various means to relieve herself, but against the want of it she has no resource. The too frequent use of food which is putrid or salted is unwholesome. Aliment of that nature vitiates the qualities of the blood, and renders it morbidly acrimonious and putrescent. In consequence of such diet the scurvy of a most dangerous and putrid kind is induced[*]. The want therefore of a suitable quantity of fresh vegetables and unsalted meat, is properly included in the causes of chronic weakness. — With regard to diet in infancy, we may observe that the milk of a nurse when in small quantity is seldom good, and by no means fit for the nourishment of a child. The want of woman's milk at the beginning of life is of dangerous consequence to the human species. If the infant be deprived of this natural food, we shall in vain seek for a substitute equally wholesome. The child from the want of human milk will be imperfectly nourished, its stomach and bowels will be disordered, and the very foundation of its constitution will be shaken.

The

[*] Lind on the scurvy.

CHRONIC WEAKNESS.

The mind and body being so closely connected, the immoderate exercise of the first disorders the latter. Excess of mental application exhausts the nervous system, and is a frequent and fatal cause of weakness. The constant exertion of the mind on any one branch of science, is more injurious to health than an equal exertion on a pleasing variety of subjects. The study of the abstruse sciences, such as mathematics, metaphysics, and the like, has often a dangerous effect on the nervous system. Studies of a lighter kind are more easily borne, but they should not be pursued beyond the bounds of discretion. It happens unfortunately that mental application is generally accompanied with a sedentary life. The mind, being wholly engrossed with the object before it, forgets its alliance with the body, and seems vainly to fancy that it can exert itself without interruption, and without any loss of time in preserving the health of that mortal fabrick within which it is ordained to dwell. The error is often discovered when it is too late to remedy its consequences. Thus the world is sometimes deprived of its brightest luminaries, whose longer existence in this life might have added dignity and happiness to mankind. Corpulency and fulness of habit is unfavorable

ble to a vigorous exercife of the mental faculties; and a weak conftitution is by no means the richeft foil for the cultivation of literature. A healthful body, whofe veffels are neither too much oppreffed with blood, nor too much contracted from the want of fluids, is the moft defirable habitation for an active foul, that is intent on the improvement of knowledge, and on the fervice of mankind.—The divine, the philofopher, the lawyer, and the phyfician, who beftow particular attention on the profeffions in which they are engaged, and who ftudy at the fame time the ufeful and ornamental collateral branches of literature, are expofed to a powerful caufe of chronic weaknefs. The practice of phyfic obliges the phyfician to join exercife to his mental labors. The profeffion of the law is extremely dangerous to a man of a weak conftitution and of a fedentary difpofition. His life is to be confidered as a life of ftudy, and therefore excefs of ftudy fhould be cautioufly avoided.

Not only exceffive labor of the mind is pernicious to the body, but various mental affections, fuch as grief, fear, and anxiety, are juftly enumerated among the moft powerful caufes of chronic weaknefs. When the mind
is

is alarmed by fear, tormented by hatred and envy, or diftreffed by grief and anxiety, the nervous energy is diminifhed, and the whole fyftem is fometimes thrown into violent agitations. The heart either ceafes to move with its natural force, or falls into fudden palpitations from the want of thofe powers which would have given it a firmer motion. Refpiration is generally retarded. The ftomach is fenfibly relaxed, and digeftion greatly difturbed. Such depreffing paffions of the mind are often fucceeded with a miferable degree of chronic weaknefs.—Even the anxiety, which arifes from the ill humor and unkind treatment of others, is deeply felt by perfons of tender minds, and confequently proves highly injurious to their bodily frames. Mankind, divefting themfelves of all felfifh and interefted views, fhould ftudy one among another to promote harmony and good will, and to cultivate thofe fentiments of mutual refpect and kindnefs, which, as they contribute to their comfort in life, contribute alfo to their health. It is not enough to avoid giving offence in matters of greater moment. The fmaller caufes of irritation to a mind of great fenfibility are, when they frequently occur, very pernicious to health, and ought therefore to be guarded

againſt

against by every one of an humane and liberal difpofition. From inattention to thefe fimple maxims of life, one may fee many perfons even of good fenfe perpetually at variance about trifling matters, and who, by living in almoft a continual ftate of uneafinefs, have greatly impaired the health of each other.

The unneceffary and imprudent ufe of remedies is injurious to the conftitution, and is a common caufe of chronic weaknefs. This fubject has been too much overlooked. I have in a late publication endeavoured to throw together fome obfervations on the abufe of medicine, with a view of promoting a more full examination into that copious and interefting fubject. For it is matter of ferious complaint that the medical art is often exercifed in fuch a manner as to injure rather than to promote the health of the human fpecies.—The unfeafonable and injudicious ufe of the lancet is extremely deftructive to health. Habitual bloodletting is productive of plethora*, and all its dangerous confequences. It is a common practice, and is frequently eftablifhed without neceffity. By this means thoughtlefs and ignorant people are led into error, and their conftitutions

* Lect. on the Mat. Med. p. 31. Inft. Pathol. Med. § 391.

ſtitutions accuſtomed to prepare more blood than is neceſſary for the purpoſes of life.—Sudorifics along with the hot regimen are unſkilfully employed in many diſtempers, both acute and chronic. Their effects and mode of operation are not always ſufficiently confidered. This abuſe has been more remarkable in former times, when the art of medicine was involved in darkneſs and obſcurity. But its bad effects in thoſe times are continued down to the preſent enlightened age, and will in future ages be yet ſeverely felt by mankind.

The unſeaſonable employment of emetics and purgatives deſtroys the tone of the ſtomach and bowels. Vomiting and purging, frequently repeated, leave thoſe organs in a relaxed ſtate, the common conſequence of an unnatural excitement. The habitual uſe of evacuants is often enjoined without neceſſity. In particular caſes indeed both emetics and purgatives are indicated, and their uſe is important. If, for example, the ſtomach from indigeſtion be loaded with impurities, a gentle emetic ought not to be neglected; for any noxious matters, contained in that organ, are extremely deſtructive of its tone. A morbid degree of coſtiveneſs too is a frequent cauſe of debility in

the inteftinal tube, and if it be not foon obviated, it is often followed with a fevere fit of the
colic.—But furely that practice is not to be
commended which, by the indifcriminate application of purgatives and emetics, relieves few
and injures many. For if we deftroy the tone
of the alimentary canal, we unavoidably reduce the vigor of the whole conftitution.

The unneceffary and imprudent ufe of ftimulants has alfo a powerful effect in diminifhing
the tone of the ftomach and inteftines. By this
abufe of medicine the action of thofe parts is
unfeafonably excited, and their native vigor is
exhaufted. Bitters and other ftrengthening remedies are dangerous, when unfkilfully employed; and inftead of reftoring vigor to the
conftitution, they deftroy its tone, and induce a
ftate of weaknefs. The long-continued employment of either ftimulants or bitters is often
productive of dangerous effects; for unlefs
thofe remedies be occafionally difcontinued,
the fymptoms of the difeafe will probably
be confirmed by the very means which
were intended to remove them.—Repeated
courfes of mercurial medicines, efpecially
when imprudently inftituted, are very prejudicial to health. The active preparations of
mercury

CHRONIC WEAKNESS. 43

mercury are extremely ſtimulating, and conſequently injurious to the ſtomach and bowels. Chronic weakneſs is frequently brought on by the unneceſſary and injudicious uſe of mercury in the treatment of the venereal diſeaſe. Mercury is an univerſal ſtimulant, but particularly adapted to encreaſe the cutaneous excretion, and to promote a diſcharge from the ſalivary glands. The active preparations, ſuch as calomel and the corroſive ſublimate, formed by the union of mercury with the mineral acids, are very apt to excite purging, and to run off by the inteſtinal tube. They are found therefore leſs certain in curing venereal complaints than the mercurial ointment *, the ſimple mercurial pill †, or the calcined mercury.

The improper uſe of ſedatives is very injurious to the ſtomach and nervous ſyſtem. Tobacco (which, though ſtimulant in its firſt operation, is afterwards ſedative) produces a waſte of ſaliva, an unnatural diſcharge of mucus from the noſtrils, tremors of the hands, want of appetite, indigeſtion, loſs of memory, and even

---

* Fordyce's Elem. of Practice, p. 361, 364.

† Duncan's Obſervations on Mercury, p. 135.

even paralytic complaints ‡. Opium, one of the moſt efficacious ſedatives, is often given imprudently, and when rendered habitual, debilitates the nervous ſyſtem, and becomes a powerful cauſe of weakneſs and irritability. I have in ſeveral inſtances known a great degree of debility and relaxation induced by the unſeaſonable uſe of opium.—It is a common error to employ heating expectorants in pulmonary complaints of an inflammatory nature, which remedies, by encreaſing the inflammatory ſtate, weaken and exhauſt the ſyſtem.—The medicines uſed to remove obſtructions of the menſes and to deſtroy worms, which are commonly called emmenagogues and anthelminthics, are often ſo injudiciouſly choſen and unſkilfully applied, as to cauſe a total deſtruction of health. They are frequently ſtrong in their own nature, and dangerouſly ſevere in their operation.—In like manner corroſives, antiſpaſmodics, emollients, antiſeptics, aſtringents, and many other ſorts of remedies are greatly abuſed, and by reducing the ſtrength of the ſyſtem, bring on chronic weakneſs.—From theſe few general facts reſpecting the abuſe of medicine, it is obvious that the practice of

‡ Theſe facts reſpecting tobacco are mentioned upon the authority of Sir John Pringle.

CHRONIC WEAKNESS.

of this art requires ftrong natural talents and particularly acute penetration; and it is equally obvious that great induftry and an extenfive liberal education, are effentials in the character of every phyfician, who upon juft ground hopes to acquit himfelf with honor in the difcharge of fo important an office.

The unnatural and imprudent treatment of pregnant and of lying-in women, is another common caufe of this lingering and troublefome diforder, which fact neceffarily leads me to make a few curfory remarks on that fubject. The practice of midwifery has been attended with the moft pernicious confequences to fociety. During a ftate of pregnancy exercife has often been imprudently forbidden, and indolence has been encouraged. Various medicines have been employed without neceffity, and without judgment. Evacuations have been too frequently inftituted with an unhappy freedom.—During labor the patient, inftead of being kept agreeably warm, has often been loaded with bedcloaths and fmothered with heat. Strong caudle has been freely adminiftered to women of an inflammatory habit, who have been unaccuftomed to the ufe of fpirituous liquors. By this means women, efpecially thofe of nervous and delicate conftitutions, are ftupified and exhaufted.

haufted. The confequences of this abufe are pain, ficknefs, fevers, floodings, and inflammations *.

The operations in midwifery have often been attempted without fkill, and performed without dexterity. The practice of turning children in the womb and delivering by force, an operation far more ferious than many feem to believe, has been too frequent, and in many cafes extremely dangerous and abfurd †.—The forceps, inftead of preferving life, has in numberlefs inftances been made the rude inftrument of deftruction. The forceps makes a dangerous and unequal preffure upon the child's head, which may prove very detrimental to its future health, and therefore fhould never be thought of but in thofe cafes where it can be employed with fafety, and is abfolutely neceffary to the prefervation of life.—After the delivery of the child, the placenta, or after-birth, has often been haftily extracted, which practice, as we fhall afterwards fhew, was attended with the moft dangerous confequences.

Sweating too after delivery has been unfortunately promoted, which contributed largely
to

* Dr. Mackenzie's Lectures on Midwifery.
† Dr. Hunter's Anatomical Lectures.

to the ruin of many vigorous conftitutions. It was an unhappy method of treatment, and has been followed with fatal effects. Nothing could have favored its continuance for fo long a period of time, but a very imperfect ftate of knowledge in this branch of medicine. Though the patient happened to efcape from fuch injudicious practice without any dangerous complaint, yet her recovery was certainly retarded.—The diet of child-bed women has been generally improper. Labor is a natural action, and ought by no means to be confidered as a difeafe. The patient deviates too much from her ordinary diet; fhe is often forced to eat againft her inclination; and thus the natural returns of appetite are prevented [*]. A very low diet is proper in fome cafes, but it is found in many others to retard the recovery and to produce weaknefs.—If diforders occur either during the time of labor, or after delivery, they have often been imprudently overlooked, or miftaken, in cafes where they might have been eafily afcertained and happily removed. When the complaint is obvious, the treatment of it has frequently been committed to unfkilful perfons.—From fuch practice in the art of mid-

---

[*] Dr. Young's Lectures on Midwifery.

midwifery, the conclufion is obvious that chronic weaknefs muft be a common confequence. Facts confirm this affertion, and too often the unfortunate mother, weak, irritable, and dejected, feels, efpecially in her declining years, the bad effects of the abufe of midwifery. It is happy for mankind, that in the prefent age vulgar prejudices are daily fubfiding, that their abfurdity is fully expofed to view, and that the practice of this ufeful and neceffary art is undertaken by men of medical erudition.

Under this head we fhall in the laft place mention acute and chronic difeafes in general, as caufes of chronic weaknefs; fome of which we fhall enumerate without much attention to method and arrangement.—Fevers, eruptive diftempers, hemorrhages, or local inflammations, particularly if there be frequent returns of thofe complaints, tend to induce a lafting weaknefs of the conftitution.— The animal frame after a fever or an eruptive diftemper may foon recover from the very great depreffion of ftrength which accompanied the difeafe; but ftill a confiderable time is required, before it perfectly attains its ufual degree of vigor. During the courfe of a fever there is a violent exertion of the animal powers, which greatly exhaufts

haufts the fyftem. That exertion is a falutary effort of nature, favoring the removal of the complaint*. The action of the heart and blood veffels is greatly increafed. The pulfe is often frequent and full, and in that cafe denotes the vigor of the living powers. Nervous and putrid fevers, obftinate intermittents, the miliary fever, the fmall-pox, the worm-fever, and fuch like maladies of long duration, bring on a ftate of chronic weaknefs.—Sudden hemorrhages have a powerful tendency to induce the fame effect. When a confiderable quantity of blood is evacuated, a greater fupply of nervous energy is required to contract the veffels in fuch manner, that their cavities may be properly adapted to their contents. From this caufe there is a want of living power in other parts of the body. Frequent and fmall hemorrhages in particular occafion a great degree of debility and relaxation †. The hemorrhoids and copious menftruation are powerful caufes of this difeafe.—Local inflammations, producing violent irritation of the fyftem, are fometimes attended with a remarkable depref-
sion

---

* See the Author's Differt. de febribus continuis medendis.

† Dr. Fordyce's Lectures on the practice of medicine.

sion of strength, and leave a great degree of chronic weakness. This effect more certainly takes place, when large evacuations of blood have been necessary to remove the inflammation, or when the inflammation has been of long continuance, or when, from the disease being mistaken, proper evacuations of blood have been neglected. Hence chronic weakness is no unfrequent consequence of pleurisies and peripneumonies, of rheumatisms, of gouty complaints, of phrensies and other local inflammations.—The dysentery, the cholera, the catarrh, and the humid asthma are productive of general weakness. In these complaints there is often a symptomatic fever, with a considerable evacuation of mucus or of bile. In the dysentery, there is a great obstruction of the intestinal tube, which, if not removed by purgatives, may terminate fatally, or at least bring on an obstinate debility of the stomach and intestines. The cholera, when attended with violent vomiting and purging, leaves great weakness of the system. The catarrh and humid asthma are disorders of the lungs, which, in consequence of their frequency, their permanency, and improper treatment along with an injudicious application of heat, favor greatly the rise and progress of chronic weakness.

There

There are also many chronic diseases of which general weakness is often an inseparable attendant. For whether sense and motion in such cases be injured,—or whether the habit of the whole body or of a great part of it be depraved, without any primary nervous complaint,—or whether the disorder be more strictly local, partis non totius corporis affectio *, the regular functions of nature are frequently interrupted, and the constitution is gradually weakened and exhausted.—A greater or less degree of chronic weakness is induced by the apoplexy and the palsy, the tetany, epilepsy, convulsions, spasmodic asthma, colic, diabetes or hysterical affection.—The same observation sometimes holds good with regard to those chronic complaints, in which the mind is so disordered as to be deprived of the use of reason, that best and noblest gift of heaven: For in melancholy and madness not only the disorder of the brain weakens the general system, but imprudent treatment of those unhappy maladies contributes not a little to the destruction of the patient's health. The unfortunate lunatic is often unnecessarily deprived of the benefit of exercise and fresh air, and he is often treated with rashness and severity.—

With

* Synop. Nosologiæ Methodicæ.

With regard to cahectic and local complaints, we may obferve that the atrophy, flefhy excrefcences, dropfical effufions, vifceral obftructions, fcrophula, teething, worms, the repulfion of certain cutaneous eruptions, the jaundice, the fcurvy, and the venereal difeafe, all frequently tend to bring on chronic weaknefs. Confiderable evacuations of bile or of mucus, tho' unaccompanied with fever, have the fame effect. Copious evacuations by ftool, the fluor albus, a difcharge from ulcers, and the gonorrhœa benigna, debilitate the fyftem. The bile and the fecreted mucus contain a confiderable proportion of the lymph of the blood, which upon juft ground is believed to be the moft nutritious part of that vital fluid. Upon this principle we can eafily account for the weaknefs, which arifes from great and continued evacuations of bile or of mucous matter.—The fuppreffion of the menfes from cold, from furprize, or from any other caufe, diminifhes the nervous energy and brings on weaknefs[*]. Such is the natural fympathy which fubfifts between the different parts of the body, that the diforders of the womb have a great influence upon the brain and nervous fyftem and deprefs their powers. Obftruction of the menftrual difcharge is always
attended

---

[*] Van Swieten Comment. in Aphor. Boerh.

CHRONIC WEAKNESS. 53

attended with want of appetite, languor, and depression; and thus that morbid affection, which is often a mere confequence, becomes a powerful caufe of chronic weaknefs.—In this place too, feveral other difeafes might have been enumerated, fuch as ruptures, dilatations of the heart and arteries; fcirrhus and cancer, morbid affections of the urinary paffages, of the womb and organa-virilia, along with a great variety of other complaints to which mankind are fubject; but which it is not neceffary to mention; as a full difcuffion of this fubject would be difproportionate to the prefent work, and lead us too far into the confideration of the caufes of death.

After thefe remarks it may not be improper to obferve that chronic weaknefs, although it is attendant on numberlefs chronic difeafes, ought not in fuch cafes to be miftaken for the original complaint, but confidered merely as fymptomatic. The treatment of the original complaint may fometimes be very different from the treatment of chronic weaknefs, and yet if we remove the firft, the patient will gradually recover from the latter. But if the primary affection were to continue, it would in many cafes be in vain to attempt the removal

of

of a fymptom. Such practice is too common, but it is very defective. It is always unhappy when any one who is a general practitioner of phyfic, but without liberal and extenfive views of his profeffion, has beftowed his attention chiefly on a fingle *complaint*, to which he is very apt to refer all ambiguous cafes, without fufficiently inveftigating their real nature and caufes. It matters not what name be given to the complaint, whether it be called the gout, a latent eryfipelas, a nervous fever, obftructions of the vifcera, or a latent miliary eruption. Phyficians fhould be warped by no prejudices, but be impartially ftrenuous in afcertaining the different difeafes of the human body, and in applying the moft fuccefsful methods of cure.

DISTINCTION

DISTINCTION and PROGNOSTIC

OF

CHRONIC WEAKNESS.

SECTION III.

HAVING given a full enumeration of the symptoms of chronic weakness, it is not neceſſary to dwell long upon the DISTINCTION of the diſeaſe. It would be difficult for any one who underſtands the nature and hiſtory of this complaint, and who is acquainted with the general doctrine of acute and chronic diſorders, to miſtake the ſymptoms of chronic weakneſs. But for the ſake of thoſe who may not have had ſufficient opportunities of acquiring the principles of their art, it may not be improper to make a few obſervations on the diſtinction of this diſeaſe.—We have mentioned obſtructions of the menſes, hemorrhoids, calculous concretions in the biliary ducts, dropſical effuſions, and
ſome

some other affections, as symptoms of chronic weakness, although they frequently constitute original complaints. But the distinction of them as symptomatic or primary, is of the utmost importance with respect to the cure; for the remedies proper to be employed, are often extremely different. The physician therefore should carefully inquire, whether chronic weakness was subsequent to those other morbid affections, or whether it existed before them. He should endeavour likewise to ascertain the particular causes of particular diseases. He should study not only their general progress, but also the manner in which they first made their appearance. By this means he will easily know in what point of view those morbid affections ought to be considered. If they precede chronic weakness, they probably constitute the original complaint. If chronic weakness first took place, and they followed as consequences, they are clearly to be regarded as symptomatic. The causes of obstructions of the menses, of the hemorrhoids, of calculous concretions and dropsical tumors, are too many and various to be separately examined into, and enumerated in this place. Nor can we enter with propriety into the consideration of the symptoms of those indispositions. But the knowledge of such particulars is useful in

disdiftinguifhing, whether thofe morbid affections are primary or fymptomatic.

Weaknefs is the predominant fymptom of palfy, but it is weaknefs attended with diminifhed fenfibility of the moving fibres. A morbid ftate of irritability, on the contrary, accompanies chronic weaknefs. Palfy is often partial, chronic weaknefs is always general. The firft frequently comes on fuddenly; the laft is gradual in its attack, and neceffarily a work of time. Palfy is often the confequence of an apopletic fit. An apoplexy may contribute to the production of chronic weaknefs, but this complaint feldom or never arifes from that caufe alone.

The hypochondriac diforder is frequently miftaken for chronic weaknefs. In fome cafes the miftake is of little moment, but in others it is extremely pernicious. The nature and proper treatment of the hypochondriac affection feems not to be generally underftood. Dr. Cullen was the firft who publicly taught the true doctrine of the complaint. The hypochondriac difeafe is commonly fuppofed to be weaknefs, attended with timidity and dejection of fpirits, without regard to the peculiar temperament of the patient. But Dr. Cullen defines it—In tempe-

H ramento

ramento melancholico dyspepsia, cum languore, torpore, metu, et mœstitia. This complaint, if it take place in a relaxed constitution, is comprehended under chronic weakness; for the symptoms and the treatment are the same. But if it occur in a person whose fibres are morbidly rigid, it is different in its nature, and requires a different method of cure. The strengthening remedies, useful in one case, are sometimes found hurtful in the other. They increase the rigidity of those fibres, which are already too rigid, and consequently aggravate the symptoms of the disease. Relaxant medicines, warm baths, and mineral waters of a similar virtue, are most serviceable in this case. By such means I have seen several patients relieved in this species of the hypochondriac complaint, who had taken a variety of tonic remedies to little purpose. Rigidity is more apt to occur in the melancholic temperament than in the sanguine. The melancholic temperament is distinguished by black hair, a black eye, and a dark complexion, with a mind slow to anger, but steady in its resentment. The sanguine temperament is the reverse. A fair complexion and an irritable mind are two of its principal characteristics. To distinguish accurately between laxity and rigidity, (a distinction of the utmost importance) the practitioner should not only attend to the temperament and particular symptoms of the complaint, but also to the nature and action of the causes. For if the causes tend to induce a rigid state of the fibres, rigidity may justly be suspected; but if the causes be such as relax the constitution, they afford a presumptive proof of relaxation and want of tone.

The hysterical affection is often attended with all the symptoms of chronic weakness. But it is distinguished from this disease by the occurrence of fits, with the sensation of a ball in the throat, arising from a spasmodic affection of that part which sometimes threatens strangulation. Convulsions, and a temporary stupor, are frequently attendant on the hysterics, a complaint in which the system generally labors under a morbid state of mobility. Indigestion, heartburn, flatulency, acidity, colic pains, palpitations of the heart, a quick respiration, a copious discharge of pale urine, timidity, changeableness of mind and dejection of spirits, are symptoms that are common to both diseases. If these cases are mistaken, the practice of course is erroneous. For if chronic weakness be considered as an hysterical affection, stimulant and antispasmodic remedies are apt to be employed, and the most effectual means of cure by restoring the strength of the constitution are overlooked or disregarded.

Chronic weakness, when accompanied with hectic symptoms, is frequently mistaken for that species of low nervous fever, which affects the patient for a considerable length of time, without ever arising to any great degree of violence. I have seen this accident happen more than once, and the method of treatment which was adopted was so opposite to the complaint, that the consequences were highly dangerous. The patients, who labored under chronic weakness, were imprudently confined to their rooms, and put on a course of heating antispasmodics and sudorifics along with the hot regimen. By this means the nervous energy was exhausted, and a sudden relaxation of the system induced. The irritability of the body was rendered so great as to exhibit appearances of an alarming nature. The distinction of these disorders is to be made, not from viewing superficially the common symptoms, such as languor and weariness, loss of appetite, pain in the head, dejection of spirits, &c. but from carefully considering the patient's constitution and temperament,

—his

—his age, sex, habit, and way of life,—the morbid causes to which he has been subjected—the season of the year, and the prevailing epidemic—the symptoms which appeared at the first commencement, and during the progress of the complaint, along with the nature, permanency, and regularity of those symptoms. The application of these general observations may be easily made, by comparing the history of chronic weakness with the history of a low nervous fever. A low nervous fever, for instance, is slow in its attack, when contrasted with the violence of an inflammatory or of a putrid fever; but it comes on much more suddenly than chronic weakness. Chronic weakness is seldom or never attended with a hectic fever at its beginning, but febrile symptoms necessarily occur at the very first attack of a low nervous fever. In this latter disease, the depression of strength and languor of countenance are more remarkable, and the febrile symptoms have a more regular appearance.

Chronic weakness is often supposed to be a latent gout, or, in the common phrase, a gout lurking in the constitution. From this error remedies are employed at random, which counteract each other, weaken the constitution, and
give

give strength and duration to the original difeafe. I have known, for example, heating fudorifics and ftimulating cordials, in confequence of this miftake, employed in chronic weaknefs to fuch excefs, as abfolutely to exhauft and ftupify the patient. But in order to diftinguifh chronic weaknefs from the gout imperfectly formed, the practitioner fhould remember, that the " gout is an hereditary difeafe, much connected with a peculiarity of temperament with which men are born, and which is founded on the original ftamina of life, communicable from father to fon." He fhould remember that, as Dr. Sydenham has juftly obferved, " the gout generally attacks perfons of advanced age, often not appearing till the thirtieth or thirty-fifth year, which may be confidered as the meridian of life. If this diftinction of the gout, drawn from the time of its attack, be lefs characteriftic in the prefent age than it formerly was, it affords one evident proof among many others, of degeneracy of conftitutional vigor." The practitioner fhould recollect that the * " gout may attack men of every fize and temperament; but it has been obferved to be particularly partial to thofe of a large fize, of a full habit, of the fanguine phlegmatic or fanguine melancholic temperament,

* Obfervations on the Abufe of Medicine.

perament, with a peculiar coarseness of the cuticle." He should consider that " the gout is more common to men, and seldom attacks females; unless being born with the temperament strongly marked, they have been more than ordinarily subject to its causes." He should remember too, that when " the gout has once made its appearance, even in an irregular form, it leaves the patient after some time, and then it generally recurs;" whereas chronic weakness, if neglected, advances slowly and gradually on, till the patient is destroyed. From these circumstances relating to the history of the gout, together with the greater suddenness of the invasion, the irregularity of the symptoms, and the nature and action of the causes, the practitioner will easily distinguish that disease at an early period, and not rashly confound it with chronic weakness.

The pyrosis, the chlorosis, and weaknesses of the stomach, often constitute a part of this complaint. The pyrosis, called in Scotland the waterbrash, is a pain in the region of the stomach, attended with an eructation of a watery insipid, or acrid humour. It is a symptom of many diseases, and particularly of those in which the stomach is affected. Its causes and nature are

not

not difficult to be afcertained.—The chlorofis is generally no other complaint than chronic weaknefs. If it is to be confidered as a diftinct difeafe, its only characteriftic fymptom is the defire of eating certain things, fuch as chalk, earth, fand, &c. which afford not fit nourifhment to the human frame. The chlorofis is a diforder which occurs in both fexes, though it is more frequent among females, and has generally, but improperly, been confined to them alone. I have feen cafes in which it has appeared in the male fex, and I can add likewife the authority of Dr. Cullen in confirmation of the fame fact.—Weaknefs of the ftomach forms an important part of the hiftory of chronic weaknefs. When it conftitutes a primary difeafe, the following is its character as given by Dr. Cullen. Ventriculi functio idiopathice turbata, per anorexiam, naufeam, vomitum, inflationem, ructum, ruminationem, cardialgiam, gaftrodyniam, et alvum plerumque aftrictam, indicata. But it feldom appears as an original difeafe, unattended with the ordinary fymptoms of chronic weaknefs. It is very often a fymptomatic affection in chronic complaints.

Before we proceed to the method of treatment, it is neceffary to confider that part of chronic

chronic weakness which is called the prognostic, and relates to the judgment made concerning the future event of the complaint. It is the business of the physician, not only to ascertain and cure diseases, but also, from a just view and comparison of circumstances, to foretel, if possible, what will be their future termination, either when the patient is left to nature, or when he is aided by the art of medicine. He does not deserve the name of a physician, who is not particularly ambitious to know with great exactness the laws of the animal economy in a sound state, as well as the general doctrine of diseases. Without an extensive knowledge of the institutions of medicine, founded not on mere idle speculation but on matters of fact, it is absolutely impossible to ascertain with any degree of probability the termination of a complaint. Ignorant of the doctrine of health and life, the practitioner can only draw weak and imperfect conclusions relative to the doctrine of diseases. Without much medical erudition he may form a superficial judgment, and solemnly prognosticate death when his patient is dying, but he will be unable to inquire into those nice discriminating circumstances, and to make with discernment those just reflections, which mark and distinguish the character of physicians.

phyficians. The prognoftic of chronic weakness muft be afcertained from the confideration of many particulars; the principal of which I shall endeavor to enumerate.

The temperament of the patient is an object of importance in regulating our judgment concerning the future tendency of the complaint. If, for example, the conftitution be purely phlegmatic, and the natural efforts of the fyftem to reftore health be weak and imperfect, the recovery is tedious and uncertain. Where nature can do little towards her own prefervation, the affiftance of art often proves inefficacious. If the patient, on the contrary, be of a chearful difpofition, and of the fanguine temperament, and if the falutary efforts of nature be regular and ftrong, there is great reafon to hope for a quick recovery. In proportion as the ftamina of life are more vigorous, the operations of nature are more powerful and effective.—If the patient be of the melancholic temperament, and his mind of a gloomy caft, he is liable to be dejected and alarmed with trivial incidents. This difpofition of mind is a great hinderance to the removal of the complaint. Dejection of fpirits, and a gloomy turn of thought, are the moft frequent and fevere

in

in the melancholic habit; for in habits of a different sort, such an unfortunate state of mind does not rise to so high a degree, nor is it of so durable a nature.—But this subject is at present involved in great difficulties. For different temperaments are combined together in different persons, and the prognostic in this particular must be regulated by a variety of circumstances. The doctrine of temperaments is capable of much improvement. While physicians considered temperaments as founded on a particular state and condition of the fluids, it was impossible that they should ever arrive at any certain knowledge in this interesting subject. But since they have now begun to make their researches more general, and to inquire likewise into the nature and properties of the living solids, their success will be greater, and their knowledge of the temperaments more accurate and substantial.

If the mind be unsteady, it is an unfavorable sign. If the patient wants resolution, he will be unable to befriend himself; and when a man is constitutionally his own enemy, it is an unthankful office to attempt to convince him of his errors. He will perhaps not be able to avoid the causes of his disorder; or, if he be prudent for one week, he will in the next be wavering in his refolutions, and in the third he will fall again into his former mifcon-duct. With regard to remedies and regimen, if he do not find great and immediate relief, he will reject the firft as unpalatable or ufelefs, and the latter he will regard as too fevere a reftraint upon his actions. Thus, from the want of perfeverance, he will not reap that advantage from the art of medicine, which a more fteady man would certainly have done.

If chronic weaknefs be complicated with chronic rheumatifm, with great irritability of the lungs and an habitual cough, or with any other chronic indifpofition, which either in fome meafure does or is improperly thought to preclude the benefit of frefh air and exercife; the cafe is often mifmanaged, the cure is retarded, and the prognoftic is unfavorable. In like manner, if the removal of chronic weaknefs be attempted at that critical period of female health, when the natural courfes are difappearing, the method of treatment is more intricate and lefs fuccefsful.

Chronic weaknefs, like moft other difeafes, is more difficult of cure in patients who are advanced

vanced in years, than in those who have the advantage of youth on their side. The animal body is so framed by nature, that, in the early periods of life, it gradually increases in height and breadth, till the evolution of all its parts be compleated, and its fibres can admit of no further distention without endangering health. At those youthful periods, a greater quantity of aliment is necessarily taken into the body than passes off by the different outlets. When man has arrived at the meridian of his days, the balance of the system is more equally maintained, and the bodily machine, in the eyes of the anatomist, is constructed upon so perfect a plan as to seem capable of continuing through ages without the smallest appearance of change. We are only made acquainted with the infirmities of years, and the natural dissolution of the human frame, by facts and experience. For so it happens in the ordinary course of things, that the body, after having attained its highest pitch of perfection, and continued in that state for some time, begins gradually to decay. The powers of nature fail, the nervous energy is diminished, the fluids are less nutrient and contain a larger proportion of earthy particles, innumerable blood-vessels are obliterated, and the fibres

be-

become more rigid *. From thefe facts, it is obvious what judgment is to be formed from the age of the patient with refpect to the termination of the difeafe. If the patient be old, the complaint too is generally of long-ftanding, and more firmly rooted in the conftitution.

If, along with general weaknefs, there be partial weaknefs to a confiderable degree, it is an omen of an unfavorable kind. Partial weakneffes are extremely difficult to remove. Remedies are not employed with equal fuccefs, when a difeafe is attended with any local affection. In fome cafes of this nature the moft efficacious means of cure cannot be ufed. Hence the danger is always increafed, when the mind is remarkably weak, timid, and apprehenfive; when the contractions of the heart are feeble; when the function of the ftomach is particularly difturbed, and digeftion much impaired; when the bowels have loft their tone; or when the kidneys are relaxed, and there is an habitual evacuation of an unnatural quantity of urine. The fame obfervation is alfo juft, if there be great weaknefs of the fe-
mind

---

* Vid. Haller. prim. Lin. p. 502.

minal ducts, attended with a copious discharge of the seminal fluid, or if the uterus be in a very relaxed state, which is indicated by frequent miscarriages, by the fluor albus, and a morbid evacuation of blood from the uterine vessels.

If chronic weakness appears unattended with any visceral obstruction, the prognostic is more favorable. But if any of the viscera be diseased, the danger of the complaint is greatly increased. A sallow unwholesome countenance, which is easily discoverable by those who are conversant among the sick, is one of the most certain signs of visceral obstructions. In some cases such a morbid state may, in its advanced stage, be ascertained by a careful examination of the part affected, whether it be the liver, the spleen, the womb, the ovary, or the mysenteric glands.

To judge rightly of the termination of the disease, it is necessary to consider the profession of the patient and his condition in life. If the profession be unwholesome and the patient be obliged to continue it, a powerful cause of the disease is constantly applied, and its effects will undoubtedly be considerable. This is an unfor-

unfortunate case, but it is one which frequently occurs. I might here have enumerated those professions which are deemed pernicious to health, but from the general rules which have been before advanced, particular cases may easily be ascertained, and just inferences deduced from just premises. Where the fortune and condition of the patient is such, that he is able to relinquish his profession, or to follow some other of a more salutary kind, there is a much fairer prospect of his recovery. Affluent circumstances too give a man an opportunity of enjoying advantages with respect to the means of recovering his health, which people of low condition cannot always procure. A man of fortune may inhabit any part of the globe, he may have the advice and regular attendance of the ablest physicians in practice, and enjoy every benefit of proper diet, of change of air, of exercise and amusement.

The practitioner should carefully weigh the causes of the disease. The obstinacy of the case is often dependent on the severity of the cause. I have given a full enumeration of the predisponent and occasional causes of chronic weakness; and, from what has been advanced on that subject, the reader will in a great measure
perceive

perceive their different degrees of power. He will find that the effects of some are small and inconsiderable in comparison of the effects of others.—If the operation of a cause be sudden, and though severe, yet not in excess, the effects of such a cause, after its removal, are seldom of so durable a nature, as when the operation of a cause has been moderate, but continued for a great length of time. Frequent and slow hemorrhages, repeated fits of the gout or rheumatism, and such like lingering complaints, generally induce a more obstinate degree of chronic weakness than a fever or an inflammation of the lungs. If a long-continued state of plethora has, by over-distention of the vessels, exhausted the tone of the system, the weakness is dangerous and extremely difficult to remove. This cause, arising from indolence and intemperance, is often found in a course of years to enervate and reduce the strongest constitutions. The tone of the nervous and vascular system becomes irreparably injured.—Excess in venery, continued for many years, induces a violent state of weakness. This cause often acts in a most powerful manner. The passion which subsists between the sexes is extremely difficult to be restrained, and therefore is frequently indulged

K without

without reaſon and without limitation. When the vigor of the body is exhauſted, the mind is ſtill apt to purſue its favorite haunts, eager in queſt of pleaſures which it can no longer enjoy.— If neglect of exerciſe, putrid air, unwholeſome food, exceſs of heat, too ſevere exerciſe either of body or mind, the unneceſſary uſe of medicines, &c. have been the cauſes of chronic weakneſs, the diſeaſe, if taken in time, is of a more remediable nature.—Frequent labors, improperly managed, bring on partial weakneſſes, and produce a troubleſome and dangerous degree of the complaint, which, as was before obſerved, is ſtrongly perceived when the patient is in the decline of life.—If chronic weakneſs occur as a ſymptom of any other chronic diſeaſe, the prognoſtic muſt in a great meaſure be drawn from the nature, cauſes, and progreſs of the primary affection.

Another important object of conſideration, reſpecting the doctrine of prognoſtics, is the nature, duration, and violence of the whole diſeaſe. If the relaxation of the muſcular fibres be great, if the nervous ſyſtem be extremely irritable and exhauſted, if the tone of the ſtomach be deſtroyed, attended with loſs of appetite, indigeſtion, pains, ſickneſs and vomiting, the caſe

is

is truly alarming. To thefe fymptoms we may add others of a moſt unfavorable kind, ſuch as a weak circulation, palpitations of the heart, fainting, a defect of nutrition, paleneſs and emaciation, reſtleſs and watchful nights, a ſallow bloated countenance, cold ſweats, relaxation of the womb and uterine diſcharges of blood, impotency and a defect of the venereal appetite, obſtructions of the viſcera, jaundice, hectic fever, lethargy, anaſarcous ſwellings and other dropſical ſymptoms. Theſe are among the fatal forerunners of diſſolution. Yet there are caſes extant in which many of the moſt dangerous ſymptoms of chronic weakneſs were preſent, and which nevertheleſs have admitted of great relief. I knew a young woman afflicted with chronic weakneſs to a high degree, complicated with tubercles in the lungs, an obſtinate cough, obſtruction of the menſes, hyſterics, a ſallow unwholeſome countenance, and general hydropic ſwellings of her face, arms, legs, and abdomen; and yet, by exerciſe, regimen, and remedies, properly adapted to her caſe, ſhe recovered her health.—But if the ſymptoms of chronic weakneſs occur in a milder form, if the conſtitution appear to have ſome vigor remaining, if the viſcera be ſound, and if the patient will prudently ſubmit to follow thoſe rules which

are

are prefcribed for his welfare, there is the greateſt reaſon to hope for ſuccefs. Yet, before a cure can be compleated, the conſtitution muſt be greatly changed, and therefore a ſudden reſtitution of health is not to be expected. In many caſes, where health cannot be perfectly reſtored, it may be greatly improved. Between the moſt vigorous and the moſt exhauſted ſtates of the conſtitution, there are many intermediate degrees of health; bleſt with which, men may attain to a good old age, and paſs their lives with happineſs to themſelves, and with benefit to ſociety. An improving appetite, a ſlower and ſtronger pulſe, together with a gradual increaſe of bodily ſtrength, are among the moſt favorable ſymptoms of returning health.

THE

… THE

METHOD OF CURE

IN

CHRONIC WEAKNESS.

SECTION IV.

HAVING confidered the fymptoms, caufes, diftinction, and prognoftic of chronic weaknefs, we come now to the METHOD OF CURE. This conftitutes the moft important part of the fubject, and therefore ought to be difcuffed with great accuracy and attention. Having had frequent opportunities of treating this difeafe, I fhall endeavor to give in detail that method of cure, which has been found by experience to be fuccefsful.

The indications of cure which we fhall lay down are three.

The

The firſt is to avoid the occaſional cauſes.

The ſecond, to obviate particular ſymptoms that aggravate the complaint. And,

The third, to reſtore the tone and vigor of the ſyſtem.

The rational practitioner will neceſſarily have in view thoſe three curative indications. In delivering the method of treatment, we ſhall endeavor without repetition to follow a regular order, as far as is conſiſtent with the nature of the ſubject. The indications above-mentioned, although they are as few and ſimple as poſſible, will, it is hoped, be found ſufficiently extenſive.

INDICATION I.

The occaſional cauſes of the diſeaſe are to be cautiouſly avoided. The obſervance of this rule is of the utmoſt importance to the ſucceſsful treatment of the complaint. No remedies will be found efficacious while the cauſes, which firſt brought on the indiſpoſition, continue to act. We ſhall therefore take notice of ſome of the principal occaſional cauſes; but

after

OF CURE.

after the remarks which we have already made on that subject in a preceding part of the essay *, it will be needless to enlarge fully on this indication.

We have said that acute and chronic diseases are often causes of chronic weakness.—With regard to the prevention of fevers and inflammations, we ought to avoid contagion, human effluvia, and imprudent exposure to cold. This caution is particularly proper when the body is heated by exercise, or weakened by luxury and debauch, and consequently more subject to be affected by those most powerful causes of fevers and inflammations. Cold alone is able to excite inflammatory fevers, whether pure or attended with local affections. Nervous and putrid fevers are produced by human effluvia and contagion. Putrefaction increases the virulence of those infectious vapors, which often exist in great abundance, and are of a very malignant nature, in jails, hospitals, workhouses, and all other confined places crouded with poor, who pay little regard to the cleanliness and ventilation of their houses. When any of those diseases occur, they should not be carelessly

* Vid. p. 21.

lefsly neglected, or committed to the hands of ignorance. The judicious application of remedies, at the beginning of a complaint, is of the utmost confequence to its fuccefsful termination. The imprudent ufe or the neglect of them at that period, may prove fo dangerous as to render all future attempts to relieve abortive and unfuccefsful.—The fame obfervations are true in general with regard to eruptive diftempers, which are brought on by cold and contagion, and increafed by the virulence and activity of putrid and human effluvia.— Hemorrhages too, morbid evacuations of mucus, bilious complaints, fuppreffions of the menfes, and numberlefs cafes of chronic difeafes which bring on chronic weaknefs, require the application of their own peculiar preventive and curative means, but prefent far too wide a field to be made the immediate objects of our inquiry †.

. Full living is a dangerous caufe of chronic weaknefs, for it induces plethora and over-diftention of the blood-veffels. In this ftate of body;

† Vid. Obferv. on the Abufe of Medicine, in which there are many facts relating to this fubject.

body, blood-letting, in proportion to the patient's ſtrength, may be occaſionally required, eſpecially when the pulſe is hard and contracted. Small bleedings even are frequently ſerviceable; for when the conſtitution is weak, a ſmall quantity of blood will over-load it, and bring on the ſymptoms of plethora. This evacuation, however, ſhould be uſed with great caution; for the loſs of a large quantity of blood ſeldom or never agrees with the patient, but often exhauſts and reduces him beyond conception. The habitual uſe of the lancet will inevitably fruſtrate the intention of the phyſician, and increaſe the malady. Temperance in diet, therefore, is to be ſtrongly recommended. The aliment, as we ſhall afterwards prove, ſhould be of a plain ſort, and taken in moderate quantity. Exceſs of animal food ſhould be avoided, as it yields too much nutriment to the body. The moderate uſe of vegetables, in proportion to the power of the digeſtive organs, ſhould be enjoined. Sumptuous tables may pleaſe the eye and gratify the palate. They are often a mark of generoſity and hoſpitality, but they are extremely injurious to health. They ſwell out the body; they bring on plethora, fatneſs, and inactivity. It is unfortunate that the pleaſures of ſocial life should be intermixed with so much allay, and that men do not govern their appetite by the rules of temperance and moderation.

As the neglect or excess of muscular motion is so highly destructive to health, exercise or gentle labor becomes absolutely necessary. "Exercise increases the flexibility of animal fibres; for flexibility is in all cases increased by flexion. It gives greater firmness to the solid matter of the body. The nutritious fluid, as applied for the purpose of nutrition, will, in consequence of its thinner parts being separated by muscular motion, become necessarily more condensed. Exercise, by increasing the action of the solids upon the fluids, tends powerfully to give such condensation to the body. The cellular membrane, a substance of so nice a texture, but of such immense extent and importance in the human economy, will doubtless be rendered much firmer by muscular motion *.—The tone and vigor of the moving fibres are increased by exercise. The nervous energy becomes greater. Habit is powerful in giving strength and facility of motion,

* Cullen's Instit. of Med. § 23.

tion *.—The circulation of the blood, in confequence of the action of the mufcles and the preffure made on the arteries and the veins, is evidently accelerated; and along with the circulation, the motion of the lymph in the lymphatic fyftem. But the effect of this preffure is moft evident on thofe veins which are furnifhed with valves †. It quickens the motion of the blood in its return to the right auricle of the heart; and of the lymph and chyle in its paffage through the lymphatic and lacteal veffels into the fubclavian vein, in order to be intimately mixed with the blood, and perfectly affimilated to its nature. The contractions of the heart and arteries neceffarily become ftronger and more frequent, which, with the confequent increafed force of refpiration, accelerate alfo the pulmonary circulation. This greater impetus of the blood through the whole fyftem caufes moft effectually a determination to the furface, and produces a free falutary difcharge of the perfpirable matter.—By exercife too, the

---

* Inftit. of Medicine, § 114. " Within certain bounds, with refpect to force, frequency and duration, the contraction of mufcles, by being repeated, is performed with more facility and force."

† Haller's Primæ Lineæ, § 63.

the appetite is increased, the tone of the stomach is restored, and the digestion highly promoted. The blood is determined from the internal viscera of the breast and abdomen, which tends to prevent as well as to remove any obstruction and unnatural enlargement of those organs.—The generating powers of heat acting more vigorously in consequence of muscular motion, increase the native heat of the body. This effect of exercise may in some measure be dependent on the greater vigor of the circulation, and elasticity of the solids.—Exercise too is powerful in obviating the plethoric fulness of the system, and preventing the dangerous consequences which arise from excess of blood. The absorption of the animal oil is considerably promoted, and corpulency and fatness effectually prevented. A state of great corpulency is very unfavorable to health. There is scarce any other state which disposes the constitution to be more frequently or more severely afflicted with diseases *.

"These are a few of the principal salutary effects of moderate exercise on the human frame.

---

* Cullen's Lectures on the Inst. of Medicine.—Vid. Gaub. Inst. Pathol. § 502, 503, 504, 505, 506, 507, 508.

frame.——Walking is well fitted for producing every beneficial change in the animal economy which has been enumerated. It is a natural and wholesome exercise †.—But where the constitution is so much debilitated as to be unable to bear walking without too great fatigue, or where the peculiar nature of the disease renders it less proper, sailing or travelling in a carriage may often be substituted in its place with advantage. These exercises are well adapted to cases of great weakness. They evidently create appetite, accelerate the circulation of the blood, determine to the surface, and promote perspiration. But where the system is vigorous, they are generally found, when used as a remedy, to be insufficient either for restoring or preserving health. Exercise in a phaeton, or in any other carriage where the patient drives himself, is, in all complaints in which the mind is dejected and apprehensive, particularly proper, because the attention is somewhat engaged, and there is less opportunity of making the malady the subject of meditation.—Exercise on horseback,

which

† Walking determines the blood in particular to the lower extremities, which in some diseases is productive of salutary consequences.

which is accompanied with confiderable mufcular motion, is extremely beneficial, and, where it can be ufed, far fuperior to the two laft-mentioned fpecies, for the purpofe of giving vigor to the conftitution. It is well fitted, not only for the prefervation of health, but for the removal of many chronic diforders, efpecially of thofe that are attended with a general weaknefs of the body and the hypochondriac affection. For the patient, from his dejection of fpirits, is apt in thefe complaints to fall into a ftate of inactivity, which is the moft certain method of continuing and increafing them. But the good effects of every different kind of exercife are in all cafes the moft evident, when the exercife is purfued with alacrity and pleafure. It is a happy circumftance in life, that exercife is often neceffary to the performance of bufinefs, in which it nearly concerns us to be active. Thofe exercifes, whether attendant on bufinefs or amufement, are the moft falutary, which are moderate, but fufficiently continued; and during the courfe of which, the perfon is in natural wholefome poftures, and breathes a cool pure air. When a patient, of a weak conftitution, has been accuftomed for fome time to gentle exercifes, he fhould, as he gains ftrength, proceed gradually

to

to make use of those in which greater muscular motion is required *. From the neglect of this caution, many continue in a state of weakness, which, without much difficulty, might at first have been easily removed †. Numbers, conscious of a sense of debility, refrain imprudently from those exercises, which would tend most succesfully to restore them to a state of health.

"By the neglect of exercise men often render themselves unfit for truly enjoying those pleasures of life, by which the Author of nature intended to promote their happiness, and to excite them to industry and activity. They also make themselves disqualified to act vigorously and succesfully in their respective stations of life, in which it was even their duty to have been more prudently attentive to the preservation of their health. They not only injure themselves, but unhappily entail on their posterity the sad effects of their indolence. But if men will not be active to preserve their own health, and do justice to themselves, it will be in vain to attempt

---

* Vid. Boerhaave's Aphor. 28; and Van Swieten's Com.

† When a person first begins to use exercise, he finds himself sometimes fatigued and disordered; but by persevering in the use of it, such effects soon disappear as the constitution recovers its strength and tone.

tempt to convince them of their error, by reminding them of the injuries done to their posterity. The neglect of exercise is particularly hurtful to children; in consequence of which the tone and vigor of their constitutions is often miserably destroyed. Often too women at the most critical periods of their lives, from certain erroneous notions which they have ignorantly embraced, injure materially their health by leading a sedentary life. By this means, they render that weakness real and great, which before was in fact much less than it appeared to the patient through the deceitful medium of the imagination *."

If the unwholesomeness of a profession has contributed much to bring on the complaint, that profession must be discontinued, otherwise the complaint cannot possibly be removed. If any business deprive a patient of his natural rest, or if it expose him to excess of heat, or to an atmosphere loaded with dust, with metallic fumes, putrid vapors, or mephitic and phlogisticated air, that business, in spite of all the efforts of art, will continue the disease. Every profession or employment, in which there is any degree of compression in consequence of

un-

* Vid. Abuse of Medicine, p. 252.

unwholesome positions, or of any other circumstance, is extremely unfit for a patient laboring under chronic weakness. Parents should be particularly attentive to the postures of children, lest, through inattention, a curvature of the spine should be induced. Children should never wear stays, but of the most pliable kind; for while the body is growing, and the bones are gristly, a deformity of person is most apt to occur. Women in general should never lace themselves so tight in their stays as to prevent the freedom of respiration, and to subject them to compression. One would at first thought imagine that the sensation induced would be so uncomfortable, as wholly to preclude the necessity of any caution of this nature. But when we see women, not only of the first fashion, but of good understanding, lace themselves so tight in their stays as to be unable to breathe without a sense of difficulty, we naturally pity them, of whatever rank or condition in life, while they purchase a false elegancy of their person at so dear a rate. How is it possible for such ladies to have regular returns of appetite, an easy digestion, and good general health, who, contrary to the most obvious laws of self-preſervation, torture themſelves in ſo ridiculous a manner. It is the misfortune of the preſent age, that ſo abſurd a faſhion is again prevailing among a ſenſible people.

If the air of a large town diſagree with a patient and weaken him, the country air is naturally to be preferred. If a damp air in low grounds is prejudicial, a dry air in an elevated ſituation will be ſerviceable. Large companies and public aſſemblies in unventilated rooms ought to be avoided, becauſe the air is heated, it is rendered relaxing, and ſurcharged with phlogiſton or inflammable principle. The frequent ventilation of rooms by opening doors and windows, is of great conſequence to the reſtoration of health, and is a practice therefore to be ſtrongly inculcated. Pure cool air is extremely ſalubrious. The fire in common ſitting rooms ſhould be ſmall in proportion to their ſize, and the air preſerved of a moderate temperature. During the time of reſt the patient ſhould lie on a matraſs in a cool ſpacious chamber, with the curtains kept continually open, and he ſhould be ſo covered as to maintain only a moderate degree of heat. He ſhould be particularly attentive not to lie too warm

OF CURE. 91

in bed, nor to encourage a copious perspiration in the morning. Such a habit, which is extremely common, produces great relaxation, and is singularly detrimental to health. It is a very general error to expose the human body too much to the action of heat, with a view to preserve it from the pernicious effects of cold. A moderate degree of cold braces and invigorates the nervous system, and is highly conducive to health. Even an infant, which absolutely requires to be kept comfortably warm, should be cautiously preserved from excess of heat. The influence of cold will be the least considerable upon those, who are frequently, but prudently exposed to its action *.

With regard to the unnecessary and imprudent use of medicines, a very common cause of chronic weakness, I shall refer my reader to a treatise of observations on that subject, which I have lately published. He will there find exposed some of the most dangerous consequences of the unseasonable and injudicious use of remedies, with remarks concerning the means of preserving health, and curing diseases.

---

* Abuse of Med. p. 210.

Too copious an evacuation of the seminal fluid should be cautiously avoided. Excess in venery will inevitably defeat every attempt to cure the complaint; yet it is a frequent cause, and difficult to be removed. What is excess in one person may be moderation in another. The exact line of just conduct in this respect is not easily to be ascertained. A prudent marriage is often of the greatest service in restoring the health of a debauchee. All allurements and artificial excitements to venery are extremely destructive of health, and should be steadily shunned by both sexes. Natural feelings and strength of constitution should alone be consulted. Rarissimus coitus (to use the words of Boerhaave) is sufficient for persons of delicate and weakly constitutions. He runs into excess, who, post veneris voluptatem, feels himself cold, faint, and weak. Etenim summam voluptatem universalis excipit virium resolutio, quæ crebro ferri nequit, quin enervat. Onanism is extremely common, particularly in public schools; and by this pernicious practice the boy ignorantly ruins his health before he arrives at years of discretion. Une quantité trop considérable de semence perdue dans les voies de la nature jette dans des maux très fâcheux; mais qui le sont bien davantage, quand la même quan-

quantité a été dissipée per des moyens contre nature. Les accidents que ceux qui s'épuisent dans un commerce naturel éprouvent, sont terribles : ceux que la masturbation entraîne, le sont bien plus *.

Over-distention of the stomach is particularly to be avoided. Nothing is more common in this complaint than for the patient to have a keen irregular appetite; but if he satisfy that appetite, his stomach is over-loaded, and indigestion is necessarily induced, attended with acidity, flatulence, and pains in the stomach and bowels. In this case the disease is often supposed by the patient to proceed wholly from indigestion, although in reality it is chronic weakness, and indigestion is only a consequence. To say that wind, or mucus, or acidity in the stomach and bowels is the primary complaint, is to mistake the effect for the cause. Over-distention of the stomach is a common error, and often followed with very disagreeable symptoms. This is another reason why public entertainments and high living, independent of their tendency to induce corpulency and fatness, are so very pernicious to health.

* L'Onanisme, p. 4.

health. Many seem to have so little notion of what is called temperance in diet, that if they are set down to a rich entertainment, they are not able to refrain from disordering themselves. After a few hours, some will be distended with wind, some will be severely afflicted with colic pains, others with the heartburn, acidity, eructation, sickness, or even vomiting. During the time of a meal, a man of a weak constitution should consider, not so much what he can eat, as what he can digest; for indigestion injures greatly the tone of the stomach. This disagreeable symptom frequently arises, not only from over-distention, but even from a moderate quantity of food which is of difficult solution. Deserts after extravagant dinners, are a dangerous temptation to those who labor under this complaint.

Excess of study is so powerful an occasional cause of chronic weakness, that very few men of learning are free from the disease. We have before observed, that excessive application of mind exhausts the nervous system. It destroys the appetite, it impedes digestion, it weakens the stomach, interrupts the process of nutrition, induces dejection of spirits, and enervates the mental faculties. As this cause of

chronic

chronic weakness acts, in proportion to the greatness of the mental exertion, with different degrees of power, it is very necessary to guard against excess of those studies, the prosecution of which requires close attention and depth of thought. Studies of this nature are often accompanied with anxiety and a temporary uneasiness, which are extremely injurious to health. A mind endowed with great acuteness and sensibility, pursues its subject with warmth and ardor; but when it feels itself bounded by its own weakness, and unable to attain the height of literary perfection to which it had vainly aspired, it struggles within itself, and exerts all its strength to break through the fetters that restrain it. When it perceives itself unqualified to accomplish its bold design, it desists from the attempt, but not without reluctance, and a sense of disappointment, joined to the humiliating consciousness of its own debility.

The deep parts of mathematics, of metaphysics, natural philosophy, logic, and such like abstruse subjects, as they require a great degree of mental exertion, are improper studies in chronic weakness. Composition of any kind, whether in verse or prose, where strength of thought,

thought, elegance of expreſſion, and correctneſs of ſtile, are attended to, is, when cloſely purſued, a laborious and unhealthful employment. Every ſtudy, in which the faculty of remembering and of recollecting is much exerted, brings on great languor and fatigue, and ſhould therefore be ſteadily avoided. I have often known chronic weakneſs occaſioned by too great mental application, and continued to an obſtinate length before the patient perceived, and was convinced of his error. Weak minds are unable to bear the purſuit of any intricate ſtudy. Natural hiſtory, the hiſtory of men and manners, rhetoric and the belles lettres, many parts of experimental and moral philoſophy, along with other eaſy ſubjects of utility and entertainment, will afford a great variety of ſtudies, which may be moderately purſued without the ſmalleſt detriment to health. Reading is far leſs tireſome than writing, for the reader often is merely paſſive, and engaged chiefly in attending to facts. The juſtneſs of this obſervation will be clearly ſeen by a conſideration of the ſtudy of the law, and the ſtudy of medicine; in both which profeſſions the knowledge of facts is the grand requiſite.

The

OF CURE.

The improper treatment of lying-in women, being a powerful cause of this disease, should be obviated by every prudent means. Of those who practise the art of midwifery, the ignorant should be instructed, the timid encouraged, and the rash convinced of the danger of their practice. The art of midwifery is an art which, in the present age, is justly held in high estimation. That is certainly an useful and a noble art, which relates to the preservation of the lives of women and of children.

During pregnancy, moderate exercise should be encouraged, unless it be contraindicated by floodings, great relaxations of the womb, or some other particular disorder, which is of real importance to require such unnatural restraint. The aliment should be mild, plain, and nutritious; for high-seasoned meats at this time are very improper. A moderate quantity of animal food is necessary, except the patient naturally loaths it; and in that case, milk and the most nutritious vegetables are required. Unnecessary evacuations, especially by * blood-letting,

* Vid. a Treatise on the Management of Pregnant and Lying-in women, &c. by Mr. White, surgeon in Manchester.

letting, are very common, but they are very pernicious to women with child.

During labor the patient should be kept agreeably warm, but the imprudent application of heat should be industriously avoided. The curtains should be open, the air cool and pure, and the circulation of it continually promoted. The attendants in the room should be few, and they should in general keep at a distance from the bed. If they be numerous, and croud about the patient, they heat the air and render it impure. By this means the woman is weakened, and the birth of the child is necessarily retarded. If the labor be severe and difficult, and the patient naturally of a relaxed constitution, an impure confined air, together with an imprudent application of heat, proves often dangerous, or even fatal in its consequences. For by such treatment the patient at last becomes exhausted; the natural labor is at a stand; violent measures are adopted; fevers, floodings, and inflammations ensue. A pure and temperate air to a woman in labor is extremely refreshing.

The general use of caudle should be abolished, as being unnatural and pernicious. The period during

during labor, as well as for some time after delivery, is critical, and not very convenient for beginning to acquire the habit of drinking wine and spirits. Wine and other stimulants should not be given during labor, except in cases where they are properly indicated. Thirst may be quenched, and the blood diluted by any weak liquor taken cool. Hot things are extremely nauseous and disagreeable. The common caudle given during labor, heats the patient, quickens the pulse, and produces pains in the head, with obstinate sickness and depression of strength. It hardly agrees even with those women, who at other times are unfortunately accustomed to the liberal use of fermented liquors.—The operations of midwifery should be performed with the greatest caution and judgment. During natural labor, the practitioner should give the necessary assistance, but he should not injure the health of the woman, nor increase her misery, by his too great officiousness under the specious pretence of relieving nature, when nature rejects his aid. The operation of turning the child should never be attempted but in cases of absolute necessity. When it is proper, it should be done in a deliberate manner and without violence. Many thousands have been destroyed by the rash and hasty hafty performance of this single operation. Instruments in midwifery should be used as seldom as possible.

When the child is born, the practitioner, according to the nature of the case, should wait half an hour, or an hour, before he extracts the placenta, or after-birth. If it be a first child, and the muscular fibres of the uterus be strongly disposed to contract, the space of half an hour may be sufficient; but if the woman has had several children, if there be no disposition to a strong contraction, and particularly if she be of a relaxed constitution and subject to floodings, the practitioner should wait near an hour before he delivers the placenta. By this means he will preserve the patient's health, and prevent great discharges of blood. We should reprobate, in the strongest manner, the hasty extraction of the after-birth, without prudently waiting a short time for the contraction of the womb and the kind assistance of nature. The ablest and most experienced practitioners * of midwifery explode, in the strongest terms, that method of procedure. The quick extraction of the after-birth is attended with an unnatural and

* Dr. Hunter, Dr. Young, Dr. Mackenzie, Dr. Harvie, Mr. White, Mr. Hamilton, &c. &c.

and depreffing pain. It is found to be a common caufe of fevers, floodings, and inflammations, which often terminate fatally. It contributes to bring on relaxations of the womb, fluor albus, mifcarriages, and habitual difcharges of blood of the moft obftinate kind. In tearing the placenta away, the uterus has been ruptured, which accident is followed with certain death. At other times a part of the after-birth has been left, and, from its ftimulus and corruption, has often been followed with dangerous confequences. When the womb contracts of itfelf, and feparates the placenta, it compreffes at the fame time thofe blood-veffels, which were the connecting medium between them. By this means the hemorrhage is inconfiderable. But when the operator tears the after-birth from the mother as foon as the child is born, the womb has not had fufficient time to contract, the blood-veffels which entered into the placenta are not compreffed, the blood therefore is difcharged in an unnatural quantity, and the conftitution of the patient moft effentially injured. There is indeed no colorable appearance of an argument to defend the immediate extraction of the placenta; and it is fomewhat ftrange that any one, in this improved ftate of midwifery, fhould, contrary to the

the general opinion of the experienced part of mankind, continue in a practice which is so painful, so-unnatural, and so pernicious.

Sweating after delivery should be avoided by every prudent means, because it relaxes the cutaneous vessels, and weakens the constitution. The patient should not be confined to live on caudle, or any such unwholesome food. She should in general wait for the natural return of appetite, and may then be indulged with her ordinary diet, when that diet has consisted of mild and simple things. After the first day or two, a little animal food may with propriety be allowed, if there be any desire for it, and no symptom of disease to contraindicate its use. When the patient before delivery has been accustomed to wine or ale, a moderate quantity of those liquors may in general be taken with impunity, and will be found far more refreshing than the common caudle. Such a diet will contribute greatly to promote a speedy and successful recovery. Milk and ripe fruits are absurdly condemned as being improper for a woman in this situation; but when the patient can relish them, and they agree with the stomach and bowels, they may be taken with safety and advantage. We shall afterwards shew that ripe fruits, moderately used,

used, are cooling and gently opening, and that they contribute to obviate the putrefcency of the fluids. They are useful in cases of floodings, and in several species of child-bed fevers. But if the patient's stomach and bowels be very weak and irritable, all fruit is to be avoided, left it produce indigestion and purging, symptoms which depress the strength and retard the recovery. Thus we see that caution is requisite in the management even of the most common things, and that what is useful and proper in one case, is hurtful and dangerous in another.

If there be no particular relaxation of the womb, nor any other accidental complaint which requires the patient to be confined to her bed, she may, in two or three days, be permitted to sit up a while, and then day after day to continue up as long as her inclination prompts and her strength will permit. When she is sufficiently recovered, so as to be able to leave her bed, and to remain up with ease and pleasure, she may, if she has been properly treated, change her room, not only with the greatest safety, but with evident advantage. It is unwholesome to be long confined in the same chamber. If the woman has not been exposed to the imprudent application of heat, and if the change

be

be made with caution, there will be no danger of her taking cold. The greateſt number of women after delivery would, if not difordered by mifmanagement, be well in the ſpace of ten or twelve days, with little or no difference in their health and appearance. The cuſtom of a month's cloſe confinement after delivery, is unnatural, and ought to be exploded, as it contributes to lay the foundation of future maladies. If the patient is afflicted with a difeafe, ſuch confinement may be neceſſary; but if her labor and recovery be natural, it will be found, particularly in the ſummer months, to be unfeafonable, and will certainly prove injurious to her health.

The infant, for the ſpace of eight or ten months, ſhould be nouriſhed principally on woman's milk. If its mother has not a ſufficient quantity, a wet nurfe ſhould be procured. By this means we provide in the beſt manner for the prefervation of the child's health, and ſhun a powerful caufe of chronic weakneſs. The nurfe ſhould be a woman of a good character, of a found conſtitution, and of an active chearful difpofition. Her milk ſhould be rich both to the eye and the palate; it ſhould not be too old; it ſhould flow with eafe, and in fufficient quantity.

quantity. To keep the child on spoon-meat alone, is an unnatural and unwholesome method of diet. To accustom it very early in life to take occasionally a little spoon-meat, is a necessary precaution by way of guarding against any accident, which might disable the child from sucking. Woman's milk is a mild animal fluid, agreeable to the palate, and well prepared by nature to nourish the delicate frame of an infant. Asses milk is the next in choice, as being light and easily digested. The milk of a cow is of a much stronger nature, and of more difficult solution. Bread is a vegetable substance, which, however well made and fermented, requires more vigorous digestive organs to animalize it and convert it into human blood. Taken by an infant too freely as diet, bread occasions indigestion, flatulence, acidity, colic pains, and sometimes purging. But though the child of a weakly woman should not be deprived of human milk, yet a mother of a weak habit should not suckle her own child. The evacuation of the milk, and the fatigue of attendance, would be more than she could bear, and consequently would sink and exhaust her. A healthful prudent mother, with a proper quantity of milk, is the best nurse, and may act in that capacity without any disadvantage to her own conſtitution. A gay irregular woman, eager in the purſuit of pleaſure and amuſement, is perpetually diſordering both herſelf and her child. A thoughtleſs negligent woman is not fit to be intruſted with ſo important a charge. A weakly woman, though incapable of ſuckling her own child, may, in imitation of the ordinary courſe of nature, have her breaſts drawn for one or two months with advantage. The evacuation of the milk is natural, and ought, after delivery, to be continued for ſome time. Weakneſs, diarrhæa, feveriſh affections, and various complaints of the breaſts, frequently attend the ſudden and imprudent ſuppreſſion of the milk.

When diſorders occur during labor, or after delivery, they ſhould, if poſſible, be removed at their firſt beginning, otherwiſe the conſequences may prove alarming. No diſeaſes are more fatal than thoſe of lying-in women, when neglected or improperly treated. An accurate knowledge of the complaint, and the timely application of remedies, are the firſt requiſites to ſucceſsful practice. The ſtate of the bowels requires particular attention, as thoſe parts are more liable after delivery to obſtructions and inflammation. If there be obſtinate coſtiveneſs and

OF CURE. 107

and colic pains, a glifter or a mild laxative is indicated. Thefe facts fhew the great connection between the art of midwifery and the art of medicine; for, however conveniently the one may be feparated in theory from the other, they are in fact united in the clofeft manner *. But it is not my intention, nor would it even be proper in this place to enter more fully into the difcuffion of the fubject of practical midwifery, and of the treatment of breeding women, a fubject indeed far too extenfive to be included within the narrow limits of this treatife.

INDICATION II.

The fecond indication is to obviate particular fymptoms which aggravate the complaint. We fhall make fome remarks here concerning indigeftion, heartburn and acidity, colic pains, coftivenefs, dejection of fpirits, and want of fleep.

1. We fhall begin then with the fymptom of indigeftion, and point out the method of obviating it as far as relates to the regulation of diet.

O 2 A

* Mr. White's Treatife on the Management of pregnant and lying-in women, &c.

A mixture of animal and vegetable food affords the moſt wholeſome nouriſhment to the human ſpecies. Providence intended us to be almoſt univerſal inhabitants of the earth. Man, for this purpoſe, is endowed with the greateſt flexibility, both of body and mind. He is capable of living in low and in mountainous countries; in countries frozen with cold or burnt up with heat. He travels from pole to pole. He viſits the Alpine mountains, the flats of Egypt, the ice of Greenland, and the burning ſands of Ethiopia. The Author of nature has ſupplied him with food wherever he goes. He has given him a conſtitution, which is nouriſhed by an immenſe variety of things. The vegetable and the animal kingdoms teem with food to ſatisfy his hunger. His teeth, his ſtomach, and his bowels, are not perfectly ſimilar in length and ſtructure to thoſe of carnivorous or herbivorous animals; but bear, in this reſpect, a reſemblance to the teeth, the ſtomach, and the bowels of animals of both kinds.

It is dangerous and unwholeſome to live on fleſh-meat alone. Such a diet has conſiderable influence on the properties and qualities of the blood. It increaſes the putreſcent tendency of that vital fluid, and renders it too much of an

alkaline

alkaline nature. There have been many examples of the scurvy produced by that cause. Dr. Gregory, a late eminent professor of medicine in the university of Edinburgh, mentions in his public lectures several cases of this kind, which fell under his own care, and were completely cured by the use of vegetables. Flesh-meat, moreover, is too stimulating and too nutritious to constitute alone the food of man. We have before taken notice that it tends to bring on plethora, for it produces too large a proportion of the coagulable lymph and globular part of the blood. It occasions heats and feverish affections, and predisposes the constitution to many diseases. Severe exercise and labor might in some measure obviate the effects here mentioned; but the consequence is, that excess of muscular motion and full living would cause so great a consumption of the vital powers, and such a continual exertion of the simple solids, as necessarily to exhaust the system, and prove the causes of an untimely death.

Vegetable food, on the contrary, is of a milder and less stimulating nature. Being acescent, it corrects putrefaction. It is less nutritious than animal food, and is therefore found too weak a diet for many constitutions. It is unne-

unneceffary, and would be generally improper, for perfons in health to live on vegetables alone; though fuch a diet would be much fafer than that which confifts intirely of animal food. There are indeed fome who have a natural antipathy to an animal diet, and would from inclination live on vegetables. Thefe fhould comply with the dictates of nature, and indulge her in her particular cravings. If they ufe gentle exercife proportioned to their diet, they often enjoy a happy ftate of health, and arrive at a good old age. But if, in any future period of their lives, this inftinctive appetite fhould change, they fhould change alfo their manner of living, and ufe along with their vegetable a moderate quantity of animal food.

Having premifed thefe general obfervations concerning diet, it will appear evident, that we fhall not recommend (as fome practitioners have done) animal food alone as proper for thofe laboring under chronic weaknefs. Such a practice, if it were generally complied with, would conduce greatly to the deftruction of health. But nature oppofes it, and, happily for mankind, fhe oppofes it with fuccefs. Reafon and experience alfo coincide with her determinations. Yet a vegetable diet is in general extremely

OF CURE.

tremely improper in chronic weakness. It produces indigestion, flatulency, pain, acidity, and purging ‡. A mixture, therefore, of animal and vegetable substances, forms the best diet in this disease.

To obviate indigestion, the aliment should be taken at every meal in moderate quantity, and of the most wholesome kind. It should be dressed in a plain manner, and eat without rich sauces.

The flesh of old animals is more alkalescent than that of young ones; it is more stimulating, and generally of quicker solution in the stomach. The flesh of young animals, compared with that of old ones, is in many cases more gelatinous, more viscid, and less perspirable. There are many examples of stomachs which can digest beef and mutton better than veal and lamb. Wild animals, whether birds or beasts, that are accustomed to a good deal of muscular action, afford in general a nourishment, which is more alkalescent, more stimulating, and more perspirable, than those which are tame, and, being under the direction of man, lead

‡ Haller Primæ Lineæ.

lead an unactive life. Animal food is more heating in proportion to the abfolute quantity of nutriment, which it contains. For this reafon, the moft nourifhing is often improper in chronic weaknefs, and if taken too freely, diforders the fyftem. Many ftomachs can digeft the weaker forts of meat, which are greatly loaded and oppreft by thofe of a more gelatinous, vifcid, and nutritious quality. A fmaller quantity of the moft nourifhing fhould fuffice. The nutritious matter of the aliment fhould always be proportioned to the ftate of the blood-veffels, refpecting fulnefs and inanition. Nutritious food, eat without appetite, and confequently without neceffity, will generally be found in this diforder to difagree with the ftomach, and to bring on hectic fymptoms.

But as different forts of animal food agree with different conftitutions, the patient muft be regulated by his appetite, and by repeated trials. Mutton, venifon, beef, lamb, and veal, are all in general wholefome meats. Pork, which contains an effential oil, difagrees with fome, and is highly valued by others. Cleghorn, in his account of the difeafes of Minorca, obferves, that, "of all the kinds of meat, none is here in fo great plenty and perfection as pork,

pork, nor is any other fo much efteemed by the natives *." Hares, rabbits, chickens, turkies, guinea-hens, woodcocks, fnipes, pheafants, partridges, quails, larks, and the like, are fubftances of eafy folution. Water fowls, fuch as the goofe, duck, teal, &c. in which there is a ftrong effential oil, do not agree with all ftomachs, though in fome cafes of chronic weaknefs they are, in confequence of their ftimulating quality, much efteemed. The pigeon affords an alkalefcent and ftimulating food, but when young is tender, and for the moft part of eafy digeftion. Meat whofe fibres are of a firm texture is, if other circumftances be equal, of more difficult folution than meat whofe fibres are tender. Animal food fhould be kept for fome time before it is ufed, that, by having undergone a flight degree of fermentation, it may be fufficiently tender, and eafy of digeftion. Tough meat is an improper food for a weak ftomach. But the meat fhould not, as is too much the prefent fafhion, be kept fo long as to become fenfibly putrid, left, by the conftant ufe of it, the quality of the blood fhould be materially changed, and the patient rendered more fubject to the fcurvy and other maladies which are

* Page 53.

are attended with putrefcency of the fluids. Salted meat is more or lefs in a putrid ftate; and if frequently ufed as diet, vitiates the human blood. Salt is by no means able to preferve animal fubftances perfectly from corruption. It only retards, it cannot ftop the progrefs of the putrid fermentation.—The hen's egg, though it is in general aliment of a good kind, yet difagrees with fome people, producing colic pains, indigeftion, and ficknefs. A hard egg is rather difficult to digeft. Pure blood is nourifhing, and in many cafes it is of eafy folution. The fat of meat is nutritious, laxative, and more foluble than the lean, but, like butter and oil, it is apt to turn rancid, and to diforder the ftomach. Roafted meat is by many thought preferable to boiled, as being more fucculent, lefs hardened, and of quicker folution ‡. Meat which is fomewhat rear affords a richer nourifhment, and is of eafier digeftion, than meat which is perfectly done, and confequently drier, firmer, and more infoluble. Meat which is fried, or baked in a pye, is of more difficult folution than that which is moderately roafted or boiled. Meat pyes are greafy and heavy, and feldom digeft well in weak ftomachs. Cold meat, efpecially

‡ Lectures on Materia Medica.

cially in warm weather, agrees better with many than hot.

Fishes are for the most part carnivorous, and feed either upon insects, or upon one another. They are in general of more tender contexture than flesh, and of more easy digestion. They are not so alkalescent, but they are sometimes gelatinous and viscid. I have known many persons with weak stomachs who could digest several species of fish better than any other animal food. There are, however, some who never eat fish with pleasure, and therefore never digest it with ease. Salmon, char, turbot, cod, scate, sturgeon, bret, pike, eel, crab, lobster, cockle, oyster, herring, sole, tench, perch, haddock, &c. afford an excellent nourishment. The eel, the salmon, the lobster, and the oyster, are sometimes found, in consequence of their viscidity, to disagree with weak people. Caviare, which is prepared from the roe of sturgeon, is oily, rancid, and unwholesome. The turtle is gelatinous, viscid, highly nutritious, little perspirable, and only fit for strong stomachs. Dr. Mandeville asserts from his own experience, that he has known many instances of stomach-complaints, in which stock-fish, a dried fish of a less nutritious quality, has been digested with ease, eafe, when the oyfter, lobfter, falmon, eel, and other vifcid and nutrient foods, have occafioned indigeftion. It feems probable that, in thefe cafes, the nutritious matter was too copious and too ftrong for the affimilating powers. Salted fifh, like other animal fubftances preferved by falt, is unwholefome, and, if ufed freely, proves hurtful to the conftitution.

Milk is a fluid of an intermediate nature between vegetable and animal food. It is not putrefcent, but turns acid by fermentation. It is an animal fubftance of a moft wholefome kind to thofe with whom it agrees. It affords a mild nourifhment, and, if not taken to excefs, gives but little ftimulus to the fyftem. In fome conftitutions milk turns four upon the ftomach, and forms a curd fo vifcid that it is very indigeftible. Several are remarkably fond of whey and butter-milk, and find them mildly nutritious, acefcent, laxative, and cooling. Butter is laxative and highly nutrient, but often turns rancid, and difagrees with the ftomach in chronic weaknefs. I know a lady who can digeft butter in a morning with eafe, but who is always difordered by it in an evening. Sound cheefe is a ftrong, infoluble, but nutritious fubftance, and fhould never be ufed

as

OF CURE.

as food, except by those who take much exercise or undergo hard labor. Unsound cheese may be eat in very small quantity, but never with a view to nutrition.

The vegetables most proper to be employed in chronic weakness should be those of easy digestion, and which, in consequence of fermentation, do not distend the stomach with fixable air.——The farinaceous vegetables, such as wheat, rye, oats, barley, rice, pease, and beans, are nourishing and wholesome food; and by the art of cookery, an art natural and peculiar to man, they are capable of being rendered agreeable to the palate in a variety of forms. Rye and oats are thought to be the most acescent and laxative: They disagree with some, and prove beneficial to others. Rice is gently astringent. Wheat made into bread, well fermented, sufficiently baked, and not too new, is a very excellent food in chronic weakness. Pease and beans contain a large quantity of fixt air, which, when extricated by fermentation, is apt to distend weak stomachs, and to bring on flatulency and colic pains.

The potatoe, turnip, colliflower, cabbage, carrot, onion, asparagus, artichoke, and other vege-

vegetables, which have undergone the action of fire before they are used, and consequently are deprived of a considerable quantity of fixt air, agree well with many constitutions. These vegetables, however, are not so wholesome and nutritious as several of the farinaceous grains, nor should they be used so freely by persons whose stomachs are weak. Potatoes, asparagus, and artichokes, are the least flatulent, and often agree in chronic weakness, when cabbage, turnips, and onions will not. Vegetables, such as celery, lettice, endive, raddish, cucumber, and melon, which have not been subjected in any respect to the action of fire, contain the whole quantity of their fixt air, are more difficult of solution, and in many cases are apt to bring on acidity, flatulency, and distention of the alimentary canal. Cabbage and cucumber are of a firmer texture than colliflower and melon; and it is found by experience that colliflower and melon are not so long retained in the stomach as cabbage and cucumber *. Cucumber, indeed, has been known to lie forty hours in that organ undigested. Colliflower, potatoes, cabbage, and carrots seldom prove laxative; but endive, lettice,

* Lectures on Materia Medica.

tice, creffes, melon, and the like, poffefs in general that quality.

Nuts, walnuts, chefnuts, piftachio nuts, fweet almonds, &c. are oily, nutritious, and agree well with many conftitutions.——The walnut is the tendereft, and moft eafy to digeft; and the filbert is juftly preferred to the common nut. They fhould be ufed frefh, or kept in a moift place, fo as to be eafily peeled.— The raw chefnut is firm, flatulent, and difficult of affimilation; but when roafted, it is tender, lefs flatulent, and of quicker folution.—All thefe vegetable fubftances fhould be eat in great moderation; for too large a quantity of them oppreffes the ftomach, excites pain, and difturbs the procefs of digeftion.

Honey and fugar are nutritious in a great degree. A faccharine principle is thought by an eminent phyfiologift to be one of the moft nutritious parts of vegetables. Both honey and fugar poffefs this faccharine principle in its moft pure and concentrated ftate. They are gently opening, efpecially honey and coarfe fugar; and where they agree, they are, if ufed in moderation, very wholefome. Many of the pernicious effects attributed to them are groundlefs.

groundlefs. When taken into the mafs of blood, they are acefcent, and correct putrefaction. As they poffefs an antifeptic quality, it is juftly doubted whether or no they injure found teeth ‡. Honey and fugar, neverthelefs, are fometimes found in chronic weaknefs to create acidity and foulnefs of the firft paffages. Honey has been obferved to bring on colic pains, and fpafmodic affections of the ftomach and bowels. I have feen feveral remarkable inftances of this kind.

The fummer fruits in general afford a mild and wholefome nourifhment. Some are more eafily digefted than others, and fome of feemingly equal goodnefs have a very different effect on different conftitutions. They poffefs a laxative quality in a high degree. Strawberries, currants, rafpberries, apricots, peaches, nectarines, figs, grapes, oranges, goofeberries, cherries, apples, and pears, are among the moft wholefome. An apple, when raw, is of a firm texture; but when roafted, it is foft, and of eafier digeftion. An apple, on account of its firmnefs, is more difficultly diffolved in the ftomach

‡ The black flaves in the Weft-India iflands, who live much on the dregs of fugar, are faid to have good teeth.

mach than a pear. The same observations are applicable also in regard to several other kinds of summer fruits. The patient, therefore, by experience must endeavor cautiously to ascertain which of them agree the best with him, and in what form and quantity they should be taken. He should know at what time of the day his stomach is in its most vigorous state, and at that time eat moderately of them. Fruit is very improper after a full meal. Strong people who use much exercise may bear it, but the weak will certainly pay dear for their imprudence in this particular. Fruit is found by some to be the most wholesome and agreeable upon an empty stomach; but there are many exceptions to this rule. In several cases it may with propriety constitute a part of any meal, but the stomach should not have been previously overloaded. Fruits preserved with sugar, as well as other sweet things, afford, if well digested, a nourishment which is very innocent in the blood-vessels; but they are apt to pall the appetite, to ferment, and produce acidity in the alimentary canal.

Notwithstanding the general utility of vegetables to the human frame, there are some constitutions so much weakened and disordered as not to be able to take them in any quantity without inconvenience. In such cases, when real, and not the effect of imagination and groundless prejudice, vegetables must be avoided, except bread, and one or two others which may be found palatable, and easy to be digested. But even in these cases, the patient, as he recovers his health, should gradually endeavor to accustom himself to the moderate use of a greater variety of vegetables; for the effects of habit on the human body are extremely great. Vegetables, like animal food *, will often disagree with one who is not accustomed to eat them, when, by a little use, they shall afterwards be esteemed by the same person as palatable and wholesome. I have been myself a witness of facts which justify this assertion.— Vegetables, as they do not tend to induce plethora, nor to excite heat and oppression, are very wholesome to persons of an inflammatory habit. They are particularly proper and grateful in hot seasons, and in hot climates, where men are less desirous of animal food. The moderate use too of ice-cream along with vege-

tables

---

* I knew a physician accustomed to live entirely on vegetables, who, in consequence of eating a small quantity of fish, was afflicted with indigestion and dizziness.

tables is frequently beneficial to the conftitution, as it takes off languor, and braces the nervous fyftem.

Tea and coffee, which are to be confidered as parts of diet, are, in confequence of their fedative quality, found to be fometimes ferviceable in chronic weaknefs, efpecially if attended with fpafmodic affections. But when they are ufed ftrong, or in too great quantity, they are often injurious to the nervous fyftem; they occafion tremors, heart-burn, acidity, watchfulnefs, and dejection of fpirits.

To over-load the ftomach with aliment, not only difturbs the procefs of digeftion, but prevents the proper returns of appetite, and neceffitates the patient frequently to take food without the fmalleft fenfation of hunger. Mr. John Hunter has by a variety of ufeful experiments afcertained, that the digeftion of aliment is quick or flow, in proportion to the keennefs or the want of appetite. If then a patient never allows time for the appetite to return, he will be fubject to indigeftion from this caufe. The ftomach and inteftines will be over-loaded, and fcarce able to move on their oppreffive contents. From this caufe too, as we fhall foon have occasion to observe, obstructions, obstinate costiveness, and colic pains are produced, which sometimes throw the intestinal tube into preternatural motions, and are followed with a diarrhœa. This disagreeable habit of eating without hunger might often be prevented by prudently waiting for the calls of nature, and then by satisfying them with moderation.

High seasoning of all kinds, as it is stimulating and pernicious to the alimentary canal, should be avoided. Pepper and ginger are the most heating and inflammatory spices, and therefore should be used with great moderation. Even common salt, which is the wholesomest, should not be taken in too large a quantity. Many are apt to eat mustard to excess. High-seasoned things are often more easy of digestion than those without seasoning, but they excite an unnatural appetite, irritate the stomach, destroy its tone, and increase the original complaint. Spices used too freely are very unwholesome. They may indeed sometimes palliate particular symptoms, but they are always detrimental to health. We do not mean to condemn the moderate use of spices, but the constant and excessive abuse of them, which is too often observable.

Acids,

Acids, particularly the native vegetable ones, moderately used in diet, are grateful to the stomach, assist the appetite, promote digestion, oppose putrefaction, and are for the most part no ways injurious to health. When used in a medicinal view, I have known them in several cases to take off the disagreeable sensation of acidity in the stomach. Pickles are to be considered as spunges of vinegar, and possessed of similar qualities with vinegar itself. But acids, where they disagree, must be steadily avoided. The too free use of them is always very pernicious in chronic weakness, for it disorders the first passages, impedes the process of nutrition, and injures the whole constitution.

It is a good habit not to eat of too many things at one meal, lest variety would provoke the appetite, and lead the thoughtless patient to gluttony and oppression.—Some kinds of animal food are more heating than others, and particularly so to particular constitutions. In this case the patient, when hectic symptoms prevail, should chuse that food which is the least stimulating to the system. Pork, calf's head, salted meats, water-fowls, salmon, herrings, rich soops, and all strong viscid and alkalescent foods, possess in general this quality in a high degree. As milk and vegetables are much lefs ftimulating than flefh-meat, the temporary ufe of them is neceffary and very ferviceable in fome cafes of chronic weaknefs.

Manducation, or the act of chewing, fhould never be performed in a flight and hafty manner. Qui, præ voracitate, cibos folidos, tenaciores, prius quam deglutiant, commandere prætermittunt, ventriculo plus faceffunt negotii, quam natura impofuit *. The learned Gaubius proceeds afterwards to enumerate the fymptoms of indigeftion, which occur in confequence of the neglect of manducation. He then juftly concludes, Hæc tamen debilibus ac defidibus magis, quam robuftis & exercitatis, eveniunt.

With regard to the frequency of taking food, we may obferve that two principal meals in a day are generally fufficient, and far preferable to four. Nocent fibi, quorum perpetuo in patinis aut poculis animus eft; ut femper pleno ventri nunquam induciæ concedantur †. Nine or ten o'clock in the morning, and four or five in the evening, are thought by fome to be the moft convenient times. Dr. Cullen is of opinion

* Gaub. p. 240. † Ibid. p. 241.

nion that the morning is the wholesomest part of the day for making a principal meal, because the animal system is the most composed, and the least liable to be affected by stimulants.— Fresh food should not be thrown into the stomach among that which is partly digested, and considerably advanced in the process of fermentation. The fresh food will retard the digestion of the old, and will itself be hurried on too fast towards a state of putrefaction. The appetite of a moderate man is generally the best director concerning the nature and quantity of his food, and it should not be cloyed with excess. A spare diet is the most favorable to health and long life.

 Victus tenuis quæ quantaque secum
 Adferat———

Children require a fuller diet than adults, and a greater frequency of meals; but their diet should consist principally of milk and vegetables, with a very small allowance of animal food.

 The too liberal use of wine, or of any spirituous liquors, accustoms the stomach to an unnatural stimulus, which increases its action, and
          conse-

consequently destroys its tone. Fermented liquors, when taken to excess, prove injurious to the whole machine, not only by over-distention of the stomach, but by the action of their narcotic power. From this cause weaknesses of the first passages, attended with acidity and indigestion, are often produced. The stomach, especially in infantile age, should be cautiously preserved from the action of strong stimulants of every kind. From the neglect of this precaution, children, at a very early period of life, are found to labor under chronic weakness, complicated with the gout and other maladies.

Fermented liquors, imprudently taken, are justly esteemed a poison. A man may be thought very sober, and yet drink a large quantity of them, so as greatly to quicken his pulse, and to excite an unnatural heat. A bottle of port or of claret, every day, is too much to be drunk by any one who prefers health to pleasure. That quantity is more particularly hurtful to a sedentary man. On the contrary, a few glasses of a good wine after dinner and after supper, are frequently serviceable in cases of chronic weakness, and will generally be found sufficient, unless the patient has been previously accustomed to drink freely. Wine thus

thus moderately used, obviates putrescency, and promotes digestion *. It gently stimulates, but does not weaken the constitution. By an excitement of the system, and by a diminution of irritability, it has been observed to render the pulse slower, and mitigate hectic heats †. We would recommend wines of a good body, such as madeira, port, claret, tent, cherry, &c. But if claret, or any other particular wine, as is sometimes the case, turns sour on the stomach, it must then be avoided.

Malt liquors, where the patient is weakened and relaxed, are generally improper. They frequently bring on flatulence, acidity, and diarrhæa. There are, however, many exceptions to this general rule. Small beer, in proper condition, is occasionally a good diluter. Ale and porter are sometimes found to agree with the stomach, to promote digestion, to open the body,

---

* Wine and water, with a little lemon juice and sugar, is sometimes found a pleasant and wholesome liquor; removing acidity and promoting digestion.

† Wine has sometimes the same effect in diminishing quickness of the pulse in nervous and putrid fevers, accompanied with great irritability. Dr. Gregory's Lectures.

body, and procure sleep. Porter is a heavy liquor, and should be taken in great moderation.

It is however observable that, in some constitutions, where chronic weakness is attended with hectic fever, the patient, at particular stages of the disease, cannot bear the smallest quantity of wine, or of any generous fermented liquor, without an increase of the hectic symptoms. In such a state of body, all spirituous liquors should be avoided, and the stomach preserved as much as possible from the action of stimulants.

In some cases neither wine nor malt liquors of any kind can be used, but they ferment, become acid, and disorder the stomach. Water with a toast in it is, in such circumstances, a proper diluent. It should be taken cold, as all warm liquors are in general relaxing and pernicious. Cold water strengthens the stomach and clears away impurities. It dilutes the blood, gives tension to the vessels, promotes the secretions, but does not heat or stimulate the system. It may sometimes be necessary to mix a little rum or brandy with the water, when a moderate stimulus is required. Spirits retard fermentation, and prevent acidity. They should

should never be taken pure, nor used but in small quantity. There is danger, left the proportion of spirits should be increased, and thus the remedy be destroyed by excess.

There are many who cannot make a meal without drinking. They find some fluid necessary to facilitate the solution of the aliment. But this is by no means a rule without exceptions. There are not a few who have a good appetite, and generally eat a hearty dinner without drinking; but who, when they take an unusual, tho' a moderate, quantity of any common liquor, are troubled with oppression of the stomach, and a sense of fulness. But the habit of not drinking, for the purpose of dilution, at a principal meal, is by no means to be recommended as a general one. We only wish to observe, that it is uncomfortable and pernicious to drink always by measure, without thirst. I have heard some people ridiculously advance, that they never were thirsty during the whole course of their lives. The answer is, that they have been too officious, they have anticipated the calls of nature, and have thought their own judgment a surer guide than instinct. By the same unnatural and pernicious method of anticipation,

cipation, they might have prevented hunger as well as thirst.

2. If, notwithstanding the necessary precautions relative to diet, the aliment should proceed too far in the process of fermentation, and the patient should be troubled with heartburn and acidity of the first passages, absorbent, demulcent, and emetic remedies will be required.

There is a variety of absorbents used in common practice. Magnesia, chalk, lime-water, and alkaline salts are the most eligible. They all unite with the acid of the stomach and intestines, and form a neutral salt. By this means they obviate acidity, which is a frequent cause of the heart-burn. Magnesia, combined with the vegetable acid, produces a neutral salt that is gently aperient. The neutral, formed by the union of chalk and the vegetable acid, is of an astringent nature. The mild alkaline salts, as they are soluble in water, and unite easily with acids, are very serviceable in these cases. Absorbents should not be used to excess; for by destroying totally the acid of the stomach, they promote a putrid tendency in the animal fluids.

With

OF CURE.

With regard to demulcent remedies, gum arabic, the extract of liquorice, and other mucilaginous substances, are useful in supplying the want of mucus, in obtunding the acid acrimony, and defending the sensible coats of the stomach and bowels.

If the acidity be great, and attended with sickness, a gentle emetic is indicated and given with advantage in chronic weakness. To clear the stomach of impurities, ipecacuan alone, or rather with a small quantity of tartar emetic, is found to answer extreamly well. In the treatment of children, tartar emetic, as it is without taste, is a most convenient remedy for this purpose. But though it is a fact, that gentle vomiting increases the tone and action of the stomach, yet emetics ought not to be too often-repeated. The imprudent repetition of these remedies will render them indisputably pernicious, by exhausting the system and disordering the stomach.

3. Colic pains are a troublesome symptom in chronic weakness. I have observed that they frequently arise from overloading the stomach and bowels with too large a quantity of food. In this case, the contents of the alimentary canal

nal become so considerable, as not to be moved along without a sense of pain and difficulty. The fixt air, which is separated from the aliment by fermentation, increases the uneasiness, fulness, and distention of the intestinal tube. The removal of this symptom consists in clearing the first passages by a gentle laxative, and in moderating the appetite in such manner as not to injure nature by an imprudent excess. The peristaltic motion of the stomach and intestines is able to force on with ease a certain quantity of aliment; but if those organs are weakened and overloaded, that motion is often too languid to perform its natural function.

Independent of this cause of the colic, which is attended with costiveness, and arises from excess of food, the stomach and bowels in chronic weakness are frequently so irritable as to be very subject to spasmodic affections and severe pains, although the body be open, or the patient even labor under a diarrhæa. We palliate or remove this symptom by antispasmodic remedies; the principal of which are opium, salt of hartshorn, musk, and æther. Opium is the most to be depended upon, though musk, æther, and salt of hartshorn have frequently the desired effect. At the same

same time we would caution againſt the unneceſſary uſe of opium, of which there is juſt cauſe to complain. The abuſe of opium tends to deſtroy the tone of the ſyſtem, to bring on a morbid irritability, and to increaſe the diſeaſe *.

4. Coſtiveneſs is the next ſymptom which falls under our conſideration. It is induced either by exceſs of food, or by food of an improper kind. It ariſes too from a diminution of the periſtaltic motion of the bowels, or from a want of bile and of other fluids ſubſervient to the purpoſes of digeſtion. Coſtiveneſs, from whatever cauſe it proceeds, is often very pernicious in chronic weakneſs. It brings on pain, anxiety, and indigeſtion.

When exceſs of food is the cauſe of coſtiveneſs, moderation, as was before taken notice of under the article of colic, is the only rational means of cure.—With regard to the quality of the aliment, the patient, in this caſe, ſhould ſtudy what things agree beſt with his conſtitution. The moderate uſe of ripe fruits and of other vegetables tends to keep the body open,

* Abuſe of Medicine, p. 277.

open, and is, when the ftomach can bear them, ferviceable to perfons of a coftive habit. We have obferved that different fruits and different vegetables agree or difagree with different patients, and that experience is the grand criterion which, in this refpect, muft determine our choice. In cafes of coftivenefs, brown bread, made of wheat mixt with rye, is, when it agrees with the ftomach, preferable to bread of a finer fort. Malt liquors are gently opening. For this reafon too, butter and the fat of meat, where they are eafily digefted, are ufeful in a few cafes of chronic weaknefs; though in others all oily fubftances, as was before faid, turn rancid in the ftomach, and are very pernicious. Butter laid on a toaft, and not melted, is more eafily digefted than butter which is melted upon it when hot, and confequently burnt in. Milk renders fome people coftive, though to others it proves laxative. Old milk is more binding than new, and boiled milk has that quality in a ftill higher degree. Cheefe fometime occafions great coftivenefs.

If the ftomach and bowels are deprived of the ftimulus of bile, on account of biliary obftructions in the gall ducts; or if there be an unnatural torpor of the inteftinal tube, with

great

great diminution of the periftaltic motion, the cautious adminiftration of laxative remedies is highly ferviceable. Such practice will immediately relieve the patient, by removing fo troublefome a fymptom.—Rhubarb is frequently employed as a laxative. It is highly extolled by fome practitioners, and abufed in the fame proportion by others. It has a naufeous tafte, but there are many patients who can take it with eafe, and find it to have the defired effect.—In fome habits oily medicines, which act with little or no ftimulus, will obviate coftivenefs. For this purpofe the caftor oil is given with fuccefs, and proves fufficiently laxative.— Manna, fena, tamarinds, cream of tartar, fulphur, lenitive electuary, jalap, neutral falts, particularly foluble tartar, Epfom falt, and tartarifed tartar, are employed. They are often varioufly combined together, and anfwer well the purpofe of keeping the body open. In this way, lenitive electuary and jalap, mixt with a little oil, are often an ufeful compofition; not difagreeable to the tafte, nor fevere in its operation. The neutral falts alone frequently difappoint the practitioner, either by not operating at all, or by purging the patient too much.—Though gentle laxatives, when they will anfwer, fhould always be preferred; yet,

S in

THE METHOD

in several instances, lenitive electuary, manna, sena, tamarinds, and other mild remedies, occasion flatulency and pains in the inteftinal tube. In some constitutions, therefore, the warmer laxatives, such as aloes and gum guaiac, are given with propriety and success. Aloes, in particular, is, in this diseaſe, a medicine of much importance. It operates principally on the larger inteftines; and, when prudently given, it seldom exceeds the intention of the practitioner. In consequence of its ftimulant effects, it is obviouſly improper in the hemorrhoids, and especially when they are attended with a descent of the rectum. Sulphur, oils, and the mildeft laxatives, which do not ftimulate the part affected, are the moft eligible in theſe cases.

When laxatives of any kind are employed in chronic weakneſs, the practitioner should study to suit them with exactness to the patient's constitution. The body should be kept open according to the nature of the case; but much purging should in general be cautiouſly avoided. Such an evacuation would weaken and increaſe the complaint. There is only an exception or two, where plethora and visceral obftructions are present, which indicate gentle purgatives.

In

In such cases Harrogate water and sea water, taken in moderate quantity, and at a proper season, are very useful and efficacious remedies. Stools of a dark clay color are frequently a sign, in this disease, of some impediment to the free passage of the bile, and indicate opening medicines. At other times they occur, not from any obstruction of the liver, but merely from want of blood, and languor of circulation, in consequence of which a sufficient quantity of bile is not secreted *. These two cases should be accurately distinguished, and not confounded together; for purging gives relief in the one, and does hurt in the other.

It may not be improper to caution here against the unnecessary use of purgative remedies; a practice so frequently detrimental to health. " The freedom with which they are sometimes employed on the most trivial occasions, would almost persuade one to believe that some were of opinion they might be given,

---

* The same thing happens to women after delivery respecting the secretion of the milk. When a woman who is very weak and emaciated, has a child, there shall be scarce any milk at all; but when she has recovered her strength, and has another child, the flow of the milk shall be found abundantly sufficient to nourish it.

ven, not only without danger, but with absolute impunity. On the contrary, purgatives of every kind are unnatural to the human constitution. They are capable of confiderably exciting the alimentary canal, and of inducing a ftate of debility, which may render it unable to difcharge the neceffary functions of the animal economy with eafe, conftancy, and vigor *." " No prudent practitioner of medicine would ever prefume to order a purgative without the cleareft evidence of its neceffity, and the faireft probability of removing a greater evil than the remedy itfelf is capable of producing †." In cafes of coftivenefs, along with extreme weaknefs, where we dare not rifk even the operation of the mildeft laxative, glifters are indicated and employed with fuccefs.

5. Dejection of fpirits is another fymptom, which requires the utmoft attention of the practitioner to palliate or remove it; for it is generally connected, in this difeafe, with alarming apprehenfions, timidity of mind, and fome degree of falfe imagination. In the proper management of this fymptom, there is an opportunity for the phyfician to fhow much judgment and addrefs.

* Abufe of Medicine, p. 74. Ibidem, p. 77.

address. The very fight of some practitioners does good to their patients. But these are men of an humane and generous disposition. They feel for their fellow-creatures in distress. Humanity forbids them to increase the uneasiness of their minds, and generosity teaches them to disdain every little consideration of interest, which is not perfectly consistent with the patient's condition in life. Their conversation, which is manly, rational, and untainted with the low deceits of a craft, both sooths and animates the mind. It affords at once entertainment and instruction, social pleasure and rules of health. The physician should study and humor the different dispositions of his patients. The careless should be bought to a sense of their situation by a cautious admonition of their danger. The timid and desponding should be encouraged into the pleasing hope of a recovery by a favorable account of their cases, and by a faithful representation of similar ones which have admitted of successful treatment. There are some patients of such a temper of mind, who, if the practitioner should perceive that they were not so ill as they imagined themselves to be, and then should honestly inform them of his sentiments, would immediately dismiss him as a man ignorant of the disease. Some patients,

tients, on the contrary, are happy when the practitioner gives the moſt favorable report of their caſe, and are diſtreſſed, beyond expreſſion, when he paints it with a gloomy aſpect. Such and ſo great are the differences of opinion, which actuate the human race. The phyſician, therefore, ſhould be a man of the world. He ſhould be able to read internal characters from external ſigns. He ſhould not ſtudy men and manners in the common ſuperficial way, which conſiſts principally of the knowledge of a few idle, but faſhionable, forms and ceremonies, that only require opportunity, ſome attention, little judgment, but no depth of underſtanding. He ſhould endeavor to penetrate at once into the mind, and to aſcertain with a cautious exactneſs the ruling paſſion. He ſhould obſerve countenances, geſtures, words, and actions, and yet ſeem as perfectly regardleſs of theſe things as if he made no obſervations upon them. He ſhould with all poſſible care gain the confidence of his patient; and if he ſhould happen to be intruſted with any family ſecrets, or to be informed of any family diſtreſſes, he ſhould act with the utmoſt regard to honor and humanity. The artful man, without ſincerity, is, in my mind, a moſt deteſtable object. He is not to be feared by a man of ſenſe, but he

is

OF CURE.

is heartily to be defpifed. The artifice employed by an honeft man is an artifice intended to promote the happinefs of fociety. A good heart has great influence on an able head.

The patient, who is afflicted with dejected fpirits, fhould have his mind conftantly engaged in bufinefs or amufement. I mention bufinefs firft, becaufe it is of the firft importance. It is bufinefs alone which can give a juft relifh to amufements. Amufements, without bufinefs, are too trifling to be the chief objects of a rational being; for the mind, in this fituation, confcious of its fuperior talents, looks down with contempt on the little things in which it finds itfelf folely engaged. Bufinefs, befides, is more important than amufements, and the mind always attends more clofely to important purfuits. If the patient is not employed in any occupation, with a view to his livelihood, there are a thoufand rational ways of fpending his time, both in improving himfelf, and in ferving mankind. In the choice of his employment, he fhould confult his own tafte, and form a judgment for himfelf. There are duties of the fublimeft fort, which a fuperior fortune enables a man to perform. There is too a variety of useful ftudies which he may profecute with

pleafure

pleafure and fuccefs. He has the world of fcience before him as matter of noble fpeculation. The earth, through the good providence of God, teems with riches for the happinefs of man. The ftudy and practice of the art of farming has employed the mind, and effectually removed dejection of fpirits. The ftudy of botany, and other branches of natural hiftory, which, when followed with alacrity, is conducive to an active life, has alfo been attended with the happieft effect. When one is purfuing fome laudable employment, innocent amufements afford a double pleafure They prevent the mind from dwelling on the difeafe. Riding, walking, fifhing, driving a fingle-horfe chair, fhooting, hunting, fcating, chearful company, light reading, cards, back-gammon, &c. are often ferviceable in dejection of fpirits. Amufements which are accompanied with frefh air, and agreeable exercife, are the moft healthful. Gentle motion puts off low fpirits. Hunting is too fevere an exercife, but the pleafure of following the hounds in fome meafure compenfates for the fatigue, and renders it, upon the whole, conducive to health. Chefs, all games, and every fpecies of gaming, where very clofe attention is paid, or where the mind, from the greatnefs of the ftake, is in perpetual anxiety,

OF CURE.

anxiety, are very pernicious.—The patient should never indulge a love of solitude; for solitude will as certainly increase his disorder, as a chearful intercourse with agreeable companions will contribute to remove it. But he ought to avoid all company in which he does not feel himself perfectly at ease, and free from restraint. Good company is generally the most easy; and ease, which has no connection with rudeness or a want of delicacy, is the first requisite of good breeding.

6. Watchfulness, or sleep that is disturbed and unrefreshing, is another symptom which the physician must particularly endeavor to obviate. It often arises from the patient's lying too many hours in bed. That kind of indulgence defeats the very end which it was intended to answer.— From this cause some are apt to wake early in the morning, and to be immediately alarmed with fears and apprehensions.—Others soon find themselves unable to sleep in the beginning of the night. Fatigued at length with their restlessness, they fall perhaps on a dose late in the morning; by which means they soon acquire the habit of lying awake in the night, and of sleeping in the day, which is a very pernicious one, and ought to be changed. The patient should not be in

bed above seven or eight hours; and whether he has rested well or not, he should constantly rise at his usual time. Sleep, like hunger, will generally return at last, where the constitution is not absurdly pampered and indulged. Exercise, and even moderate labor, are excellent means for procuring sleep, with the want of which the active and laborious part of mankind are seldom troubled.

If the patient make a plentiful meal at supper, the consequence in many cases will be a general sense of uneasiness, nocturnal heats, oppression of the stomach, and want of sleep, or sleep unrefreshing and interrupted with frightful dreams. But this observation holds good only during the presence of a disease; for when a man is in health and exercise, a plentiful supper, if he be hungry, may be taken without any disadvantage. Sleep, with a full stomach, is neither unnatural nor unwholesome. On the continent there are whole nations among whom the supper has been the principal meal for ages past, and the inhabitants have not found any just cause to change this part of their method of living. The brute creation, almost without exception, go to rest after a full meal; and however imperfect the analogy may be in many other cases, it is in this evidently strong and just. Man too, like other animals,

finds

finds himself, after a plentiful meal, to have naturally a disposition to rest, and it can hardly be supposed improper and unwholesome to follow the undoubted guidance of nature*. Reason, in this instance, is of inferior authority. I have the honor of being acquainted with several eminent physicians, who maintain it as a fact founded on observation, that digestion is performed in as perfect a manner during sleep, as at any other time. I know many people in health, who take a hearty supper without the smallest inconvenience. Numerous facts of this kind are manifest to the most superficial observer.—But, notwithstanding these remarks, I would by no means be understood to recommend the supper as a principal meal. I am confident such a habit is often very hurtful to the constitution. For though a man in health and in exercise may eat freely at supper, yet one who is not in health, or who, if in health, is not in exercise, will certainly be injured by it. When I speak of the exercise in consequence of which a man may be allowed to

---

* Sleep after dinner is not unwholesome, provided the constitution requires it, and the person has not been too many hours in bed. But when any one lies during the night eight hours in bed, sleep after dinner is an absurd indulgence, which will seldom answer any good purpose, and may often prove hurtful.

eat suppers, I do not mean a trivial saunter, or loitering for an hour or two in an easy carriage, but exercise which approaches to moderate labor. If a person be in health, and only uses gentle exercise, suppers will contribute to overload his constitution, to induce plethora, over-distention of the vessels, and an unhappy train of consequences.

When, notwithstanding a proper attention to exercise and regimen in every respect, there is still an obstinate watchfulness, antispasmodics and opiates are required. But opiates should in this case be used with caution, and never without absolute necessity. If the dose be too large, the patient is apt to wake in the morning sick, faint, and dejected.—We may just hint too in this place, that if any particular symptom of chronic weakness should disturb the patient in the night, the natural return of sleep will depend on the removal of the irritating cause, whether local or more general, and whether connected with pain or with anxiety.

There are several other symptoms, which seem to require a full and separate consideration, such as obstinate head-achs, vomiting, chronic rheumatism, worms, diarrhœa, feverishness, obstruction

tion of the menses, biliary concretions, &c. But the removal of these, as symptoms of chronic weakness, depends principally on restoring the tone of the system, and therefore we shall have occasion here to make only a very few observations upon them.

Obstinate head-achs are sometimes relieved by topical bleeding, by shaving the head, by blisters, issues, setons, warm fomentations, antispasmodics, mild sudorifics, &c.—Frequent vomiting requires a strict observance of the rules laid down for the prevention of indigestion. Gentle emetics, absorbents, laxatives, saline mixtures, cordials, aromatics, opiates and other antispasmodics, may be occasionally indicated.—The chronic rheumatism is sometimes relieved by volatile liniments, blisters, leeches, frictions, gum guaiac, the oil of turpentine, decoctions of the woods, neutral salts, antimonials, Dover's powder, and other gentle sudorifics.

Worms, when they occur in consequence of relaxation in the stomach and bowels, are a symptom of chronic weakness, and are evidently to be overcome by strengthening the whole constitution. We may just take notice, that the powder of tin is a valuable remedy in this case.
Mild

Mild mercurials, and purgatives too are sometimes required; but they are often used with imprudence, and prove extremely pernicious.

A diarrhæa, according to its peculiar nature, is to be removed by emetics, laxatives, absorbents, demulcents, cordials, and opiates. Laxatives should not, as is too frequently the case, be promiscuously used without indication. They are indicated and given with success when there is any morbid matter in the bowels, which ought to be removed. Rhubarb, in this case, is thought by many to be a convenient laxative. When absorbents are necessary, chalk is to be preferred, as it proves gently astringent. Aromatics, infused in red wine, are useful cordials. But, when the diarrhæa is connected with an irritable state of the intestinal tube, opium is in general the most important remedy.

Feverishness from cold is a very frequent occurrence, and aggravates the symptoms of chronic weakness. The means which are adapted to remove it are many and various. The cooling antiphlogistic regimen, but not always in its fullest extent. The saline mixture, nitre, and the spirit of Minderirus. Blood-letting, in cases of plethora, whether venous or arterial. Blisters, especially

especially when there is any local affection. Laxatives, with a view only to keep the body open, except when plethora is present. Emetics, either in full or divided doses, but particularly tartar emetic and James's powder, which, when administered at the first attack, are frequently succesful in removing the fever. Wine and cordial stimulants. Mild sudorifics, employed without the hot regimen. Opium, and other sedatives, given for the purpose of removing the symptoms of irritation. Tonic and strengthening remedies, the principal of which is the Peruvian bark.

When the obstruction of the menses is to be considered as a primary disease, it is not an object of our present inquiry. When it occurs as a symptom of chronic weakness, it is most effectually removed by remedies which restore the tone of the system. Warm and stimulating laxatives too are sometimes used with peculiar propriety, just at the period when the menses are naturally expected. If the menses should at last return with pain and difficulty, warm fomentations, pediluvium, opium, musk, and other antispasmodics are indicated.—Calculous concretions in the biliary ducts, when they occur as symptomatic in chronic weakness, require the general cure of
the

the complaint. Laxatives, emetics, antiscorbutic juices, absorbents, opiates, antispasmodics, and corroborants, are found serviceable. Opiates are principally to be employed, when, from a spasmodic affection, there is pain in the region of the liver. But when this symptom takes place, emetics are evidently dangerous, and blood-letting in full habits is often useful.

INDICATION III.

We come now to the last part of the cure, in which the indication is to restore the tone and vigor of the system. This important change is to be made by the use of astringents, stimulants, and tonics. These remedies, when prudently administered, strengthen the system. But they are often employed in such an improper manner, as to disagree with the patient, and to increase the disease. The prudent exhibition of a remedy is of the utmost consequence to its successful operation. But ignorance and prudence are perpetually at variance. They oppose each other with warmth, and, by the unhappy conflict, reason is degraded, society is injured, the order and harmony of things is strangely perverted. Astringents, stimulants, and tonics, being all strengthening medicines, it is difficult to draw the

exact

exact line of distinction between them. Astringents, which increase the firmness and cohesion of the simple solids, do necessarily increase the tone and contractile force of the living fibres. Stimulants and tonics likewise, which act principally on the living fibres, have considerable influence on the simple solids.

Before we proceed to inquire into the particular use and misapplication of astringents, stimulants, and tonics, it may just be hinted, that we have already treated of the good effects of exercise and of cold air, which are powerful strengtheners of the system. I must repeat it, that excess of warmth, and the neglect of exercise, will certainly frustrate every attempt towards a cure. Good aliment, if it be not well digested, will not afford proper nourishment to the body. The best corroborating medicines will not restore the tone of a weakened constitution, unless the stomach be able to extract their virtues. But the good effects of them will never be completely obtained by any one, without the assistance of cold air and exercise. For this reason, whatever prevents the application of cold air and the use of exercise, is extremely unfavorable to the cure of chronic weakness. When the patient's indolence and caprice hinder the successful operation of remedies, the humane mind is naturally hurt, and pity is moved at the fight of diftrefs, which might otherwife have been happily relieved.

ASTRINGENT remedies are found efficacious in the removal of chronic weaknefs. They give ftrength and firmnefs to the fimple folids, and confequently affift the action of the mufcular fibres. They invigorate the contractile power of the heart and arteries. They reftore tone to the ftomach and bowels; they give appetite, moderate the procefs of fermentation, prevent acidity, and promote digeftion.

The uva urfi, the bark of the oak, campeachy wood, tormentil and biftort, are frequently given with this view, and are efficacious aftringents. The boles, dragon's blood, and japan earth, are faid to be fometimes ferviceable, but their operation is weak and uncertain.

Alum is a powerful aftringent. It is a compofition formed by the union of an argillacious earth with the vitriolic acid. It is a natural production, but one which may be eafily imitated by art. Applied to the lips, it renders them pale, by producing a conftriction of their veffels.

sels. It possesses the power of hardening animal substances, and of preserving them from corruption *. It is a remedy which is often employed with great advantage in chronic weakness. Its efficacy is obvious in relaxations of the stomach and bowels †, and of the urinary passages. It is particularly serviceable, when there is a local relaxation of the uterine vessels, attended with a flooding or too copious a discharge of the menses. Alum readily dissolves in aqueous fluids, and, when properly diluted, enters into the circulatory system, and is applied to every part of the body. It is a remedy of an active operation, and may in many cases be taken in considerable doses. But alum will by no means agree with every constitution, for it is sometimes found to irritate the alimentary canal, and to excite pain and sickness.

* Vid. Sir John Pringle's Observations on Septics and Antiseptics.

† Percival's Essays, vol. 2, p. 196. "This remedy, when continued for a sufficient length of time, seems to abate flatulence, to obviate spasm, to improve the appetite, and to strengthen the organs of digestion." Dr. Percival likewise mentions several cases of obstinate colics, which were cured by the use of alum.

Galls, given in moderate dofes, have been employed with fuccefs in great relaxations of the fyftem, and particularly in uterine hemorrhages which have endangered life*. They poffefs ftrong ftiptic qualities, and a powerful remedy, ufed with judgment, is requifite in a dangerous difeafe.—The fugar of lead, fo called from its fweetnefs, being a compofition of lead and a vegetable acid, has alfo been recommended in fimilar cafes. It is indeed a moft powerful aftringent, but its pernicious effects on the nervous fyftem, have deterred the regular practitioner from ufing it with any degree of freedom.

STIMULANTS are a clafs of remedies that are extremely numerous. The following are thofe which are in general ufe among the ableft phyficians, and many of them feem evidently poffeffed alfo of antifpafmodic virtues. Peppermint, cinnamon, lavender, canella alba, cloves, ginger, camphor, gum guaiac, Virginian fnakeroot, balfams, muftard, horfe-raddifh, caftor, afafætida, æther, falt of hartfhorn, wine, fpirits, common falt, &c. But it is unneceffary to enlarge either on the chymical compofition, or the natural hiftory of thefe remedies; for they are fubjects

---

* Dr. Fordice's Lectures on the Practice of Phyfic.

jects already well discussed in books of chymistry, and of the materia medica.

The prudent use of stimulants often affords much relief in cases of chronic weakness, especially when that disease is accompanied with great languor and torpor of the living powers. Stimulants excite the action of the nervous system. They accelerate the circulation, promote the discharge by the skin, and eliminate from the blood those putrescent particles, which are often retained in consequence of languor and debility. They increase the peristaltic motion of the alimentary tube; they retard fermentation, prevent acidity, and forward the digestion of the aliment. By this means the appetite is improved, and the process of nutrition carried on in a more perfect manner. I have already observed, that the moderate use of spices along with our aliment, is not only admissible, but evidently proper in chronic weakness.

Stimulants may be united with tonics, whose salutary operation they sometimes promote, as they tend to prevent them from producing any sense of weight and oppression in the stomach.—Hot inflammatory stimulants should be employed with caution; for when used too freely, they
cause

cause a morbid circulation of the blood, excite an unnatural heat, and injure materially the constitution. I have known them indeed given in so acrid a state, as to excoriate the patient's mouth and throat. The reader will easily judge how dangerous the effects of such a remedy must be, on so delicate an organ as the human stomach. It seemed as if the practitioner was of opinion, that the acrimony of his medicine would insure its success.—No stimulants should ever be employed for a great length of time without intermission, for the long-continued use of them is a notorious abuse of medicine.

In some constitutions where the hectic fever is strongly prevalent, stimulants of every kind, especially in hot weather, are found to heat and disagree with the patient. I have seen several instances, in which even the mildest stimulants have produced this effect. In these peculiarities of temperament, the physician, perceiving that his patient is of an inflammatory habit, will naturally desist from the use of stimulants, and endeavor to alleviate his sufferings, by a practice founded somewhat on the cooling antiphlogistic plan, but without the use of unnecessary evacuations.

Tonics

Tonics are the laſt remedies that we ſhall have occaſion to mention. They are juſtly ranked among the moſt valuable that are uſed in the cure of chronic weakneſs. They obviate the laxity of the habit, and tend to remove the very cauſe of the complaint. They ſtrengthen and conſolidate. They increaſe the nervous influence, and conſequently facilitate the performance of the different functions of the animal economy. They invigorate the contractions of the heart and arteries. They increaſe the tone of the alimentary canal, and promote the digeſtion of the food and the proceſs of nutrition. They obviate a morbid exceſs of general irritability, which diſtreſſes the patient, and renders him ſubject to have the eaſe of his mind and body diſturbed by every trivial incident. They take off a ſenſation of trembling about the heart and ſtomach, which is a frequent and diſtreſſing ſymptom in this complaint. " If coſtiveneſs ariſe from weakneſs of the alimentary canal, they tend to remove it. If a diarrhæa occur from irritability and relaxation, they check the diſcharge by directly obviating the cauſe. If colic pains, loſs of appetite, frequent vomiting, palpitations of the heart, dejection of ſpirits, obſtruction of the menſes, defective perſpiration, &c. are the conſequences of weakneſs and mobility, no remedies are so well adapted for the removal of those morbid affections *."

The tonics to be employed in chronic weakness are cold bathing, the preparations of steel, and chalybeate waters, bitters, and the Peruvian bark.

Cold bathing is an excellent remedy. The application of the water is made to the surface of the body, but by means of the general sympathy which takes place, its tonic effects are readily communicated to the most interior parts. It strengthens in particular the system of the absorbent and exhalant vessels, and moderates too copious an evacuation by the cutaneous pores. It is a powerful bracer, and very serviceable in the removal of irritability. Cold bathing destroys too that unnatural delicacy of constitution which arises from excess of heat, and is so extremely distressing to the patient. For while that delicacy subsists, his happiness is the sport of every wind, and the instability of his health keeps pace with the changeableness of the weather. Such a state of body, which, from the inconsiderateness

---

* Abuse of Medicine, p. 30.

ness of mankind is frequent beyond expression, renders the person a true object of compassion.

The degree of coldness in the water should be proportioned to the patient's strength of constitution. If the water be too cold, it will prevent that salutary re-action of the heart and arteries, which is indicated after bathing by the sensation of a gentle universal warmth. To promote this re-action of the vascular and nervous systems, the patient should have acquired by exercise a moderate degree of heat before he goes into the water. It is often proper, in cases of great weakness, to begin with a temperate bath, and afterwards to proceed to the use of one which is colder. For this purpose the waters of Buxton and Matlock, in Derbyshire, are often highly serviceable in chronic weakness.

Bathing in the sea, when it is properly indicated, is found in fact to be more efficacious than bathing in the cold bath. The water of the sea is impregnated with salts which stimulate the surface, and contribute to excite the re-action of the system. The greater specific gravity of the sea water, gives a greater pressure upon the surface of the body. The sea breezes too promote appetite,

appetite, assist digestion, and invigorate the constitution.

But whether the water be salt or fresh, the frequency of bathing and the time of continuing in it, can only be determined by the nature and symptoms of the disease. To bathe three or four times a week is generally sufficient. A patient who is greatly debilitated should not bathe too frequently, and he should remain in the water but a single moment. One of greater strength may use the bath more freely, and continue in it for a few minutes. Cold bathing is particularly adapted to remove the lingering pains of chronic rheumatism, which are a common attendant on chronic weakness. Swimming in a temperate water is an useful exercise, requiring the action of almost every muscle. It may be employed too at a season of the year, when the warmth of the weather will not admit exercises of a different kind.

The preparations of steel are medicines which are highly valued in this disease. They are safe as well as efficacious tonics; and in this respect, therefore, preferable in general to the preparations of copper, which nevertheless have of late been recommended by several eminent physicians,

ans in particular cafes of chronic weaknefs. From a chymical analyfis of the human body, a fmall portion of iron is found by the accurate chymift to be one of its conftituent parts.

Steel, when rendered foluble in aqueous fluids, by means of its union with an acid, has a fuccefsful operation in ftrengthening the fyftem. The falt of fteel, a neutral in which fteel and the vitriolic acid are combined, is a valuable remedy, and capable of producing very good effects. It will diffolve in water, enter the veffels, mix with the blood, and be diftributed over the whole fyftem. When fteel is finely powdered and taken in fubftance, a portion of it is diffolved by the vegetable acid which is in the firft paffages, and by this folution its action on the human body is promoted.—The effects of fteel are very general in removing all the fymptons of chronic weaknefs. It is a medicine well adapted to obviate relaxations of the womb, to remove obftructions of the menfes, or to check preternatural uterine difcharges, whether of mucus or of blood.

For the fame intentions, the ufe of chalybeate waters are ftrongly recommended, and where there is no venous or arterial plethora, they are remedies which are extremely ufeful in reftoring the tone of the syftem. The cold water in which the steel is contained, contributes to the efficacy of the medicine. Mineral waters of the chalybeate kind are particularly serviceable in the glandular obstructions of children and young people, which frequently take place in very weak and relaxed constitutions. In such cases mineral waters, possessed of a purgative quality, are frequently used, but never without pernicious consequences. Chalybeate waters support the strength of the patient; and, by penetrating into the minutest vessels, they tend to wash out of the system every species of acrimony, which is capable of irritating the tender and delicate substance of the lymphatic glands.

The chalybeate water of Scarbrough is of singular utility in chronic weakness, and is justly celebrated in the present age. Scarbrough has the united advantages of a good situation, of a wholesome air and a neighbouring sea. Other steel mineral waters, such as those of Spa, Pyrmont, Harrogate, &c. are valuable and efficacious medicines. The artificial Pyrmont water, which is made by impregnating water with fixt air and iron, has of late been frequently employed with success. The fixt air tends to moderate the fermentation in the stomach,

OF CURE.

mach, and to prevent putrefaction. The Bath waters too are possessed of a chalybeate quality *, and, from their peculiar nature, are at once both stimulant and tonic. They are often of great service in chronic weakness, and particularly when the stomach and bowels are much diseased, the appetite depraved, and the digestion weak †.

Besides the intrinsic efficacy of these mineral waters, the patient, who resorts to public places, has the benefit of change of air, exercise, relaxation from business, chearful and agreeable company. These circumstances, taken together, are of importance in promoting the recovery of health. Chearful company is often particularly serviceable to a mind weakened and dejected. The exercise of travelling is, for the most part, as pleasant as it is useful; and a freedom from the anxiety of business is frequently not to be obtained, but by a change of place, and a removal from the hurrying scenes of life.

Bitters, and the Peruvian bark, are the last tonic medicines we shall mention. They are valuable remedies

* Vid. Falconer on Bath Waters, p. 291.
† Ibid. p. 343.

remedies in the cure of chronic weaknefs. They contribute much towards the removal of the complaint. They increafe the tone of the fyftem in a high degree, and facilitate the performance of the different functions of the body, whether animal, vital, or natural. By increafing the tone of the circulatory fyftem, they obviate ficknefs and fainting, which take place in confequence of weaknefs and irritability. They often relieve in cafes where hectic fymptoms are evidently prefent, tho' fometimes hectic fymptoms, efpecially in very warm weather, are increafed by thefe remedies, and contraindicate their ufe. The bitters moft commonly employed, are gentian, chamomile, tanfy, orange peel, fima ruba, zeduary, eleutheria, and columbo root. The Peruvian bark is experienced to be one of the moft ufeful remedies in chronic weaknefs. But it is a vulgar error to fuppofe that the bark will agree with every conftitution. It is fometimes found of little or no fervice in this difeafe, efpecially in fome dry, lean, and bilious habits. Bitters and the bark may be taken in various forms, as is moft agreeable to the patient. The decoction, the infufion, the extract, and the powder, are frequently employed. The cold infufion of the bark is ftronger than the decoction; but the powder, when it agrees with the ftomach, is preferable to

any

OF CURE. 167

any other preparation. These remedies are frequently given along with the vitriolic and other mineral acids, all of which are observed to retard fermentation, to prevent acidity, produce appetite, and promote digestion.

With these remarks concerning tonics, I shall conclude this treatise on chronic weakness. The subject of it is undoubtedly important, however imperfect the execution may be. On this point candid and judicious readers will form an opinion for themselves, and their opinion ought always to be considered as decisive. The author may truly affirm, that he has spared no labor to avoid obscurity and the misrepresentation of facts; and that, besides his own observations on the disease, he has had frequent opportunities of hearing the sentiments, and of seeing the practice of several eminent physicians, whose genius and erudition do honor to the age in which they live, and whose names will be most respectfully transmitted to posterity.

During the course of these observations, we have seen what various means are to be employed in the cure of chronic weakness. Different remedies are requisite in different cases, whether they be intended to palliate particular symptoms,

or

or to eradicate the complaint. An injudicious choice of them fruſtrates the intentions of the phyſician, and leaves the unhappy patient to ſtruggle on with the miſeries of his diſeaſe. Such is the variety, and ſuch are the peculiarities of conſtitutions, that a remedy, which relieves one perſon, will injure another. It is therefore of great importance that the phyſician ſhould be extremely attentive to acquire an exact hiſtory and knowledge of the caſe, and judiciouſly to ſelect thoſe medicines which are beſt adapted to the patient's temperament, and to the peculiar ſymptoms and nature of the affection. The moſt efficacious remedies ſhould be given in the moſt ſimple, elegant, and agreeable forms. Elegance of preſcription, without ſimplicity, is not ſufficient. Simplicity of preſcription is of the firſt importance towards ſuccefsfully aſcertaining the reſpective virtues of different medicines.—Beſides the neceſſary application of remedies, we have found that a ſtrict attention to regimen is of the utmoſt confequence. Thoſe practitioners are deceived, who aſſert that regimen is little to be regarded in chronic weakneſs. We would fain hope there are but few who are ſo blind to the real welfare of their patients. Without a proper regimen, the operation of remedies will diſappoint the otherwiſe reaſonable expectations of the

phyſician.

physician.—The patient, knowing the abilities of the practitioner, and having entered on a course of proper remedies, should submit himself to his care, with full confidence of obtaining all the relief which the art of medicine can safely procure. He should remember that, considering the obstinacy and previous duration of his complaint, a sudden change from a state of morbid relaxation to a state of natural tension, however desirable at first sight it may seem, is not only impossible in the nature of things, but were it even possible, would, in all probability, be attended with the greatest danger.

THE END.

www.ingramcontent.com/pod-product-compliance
Lightning Source LLC
Chambersburg PA
CBHW032151160426
43197CB00008B/865